OCS Study MMS 2005-036

ALASKA OCS REGION

TENTH INFORMATION TRANSFER MEETING
and
BARROW INFORMATION UPDATE MEETING

Final Proceedings

March 14, 15, and 16, 2005
Anchorage, Alaska

March 18, 2005
Barrow, Alaska

Prepared for:

U.S. Department of the Interior
Minerals Management Service
Alaska OCS Region
3801 Centerpoint Drive, Suite 500
Anchorage, Alaska 99503-5823

Under Contract No. 1435-01-02-CT-31150

Prepared by:

MBC *Applied Environmental Sciences*
3000 Redhill Avenue
Costa Mesa, California 92626

June 2005

DISCLAIMER

This report has been reviewed by the Alaska OCS Region, Minerals Management Service, U.S. Department of the Interior and approved for publication. The opinions, findings, conclusions, or recommendations expressed in the report are those of the authors, and do not necessarily reflect the view of the Minerals Management Service. Mention of trade names for commercial products does not constitute endorsement or recommendations for use. This report is exempt from review by the Minerals Management Service Technical Publication Unit and Regional Editor.

CITATION

Suggested citation:

MBC Applied Environmental Sciences. 2005. Proceedings of the Tenth MMS Information Transfer Meeting and Barrow Information Update Meeting. OCS Study MMS 2005-036. Prepared by MBC Applied Environmental Sciences, Costa Mesa, CA. Prepared for the U.S. Dept. of the Interior, Minerals Management Service, Alaska OCS Region, Anchorage, AK. 112 pp. plus attachments.

TABLE OF CONTENTS

BIOLOGY   **Page**

PROTECTED SPECIES

SOCIAL SCIENCE AND ECONOMICS

- Presentation also given at the Barrow Information Update Meeting. Note that after the summary of a presentation "Discussion" means "Discussion from the Anchorage ITM." Otherwise "Discussion from the Barrow IUM" is specified.

LIST OF FIGURES AND TABLES

                                                                                                              Page

Attachments
        I Agendas
                Information Transfer Meeting in Anchorage
                Information Update Meeting in Barrow

        II Attendee Lists
                Information Transfer Meeting in Anchorage
                Information Update Meeting in Barrow

Introduction

WELCOME TO THE ITM AND
THE ALASKA ENVIRONMENTAL STUDIES PROGRAM

Cleve Cowles, Ph.D.

Chief, Environmental Studies Section
MMS, Alaska OCS Region
3801 Centerpoint Drive, Anchorage, AK 99503

It is very gratifying to see so many of you here, considering the competition for this meeting. Some of you from this part of the country are aware of only a couple of weeks ago we finished off the Fur Rendezvous Sprint races and about nine days ago the Iditarod started. Folks in this town are just dog-tired and it is a surprise to see you here. There is that great Alaskan spirit, bright-eyed, and bushy-tailed, out on the trail and here. So welcome again.

My name is Cleve Cowles and I am the chief of the Environmental Studies Section for the MMS Alaska OCS Region. The goals of our MMS Mission-oriented studies program are:

- To establish information needed for prediction, assessment, and management of potential effects on the human, marine, and coastal environment related to Outer Continental Shelf oil and gas activities,
- To enhance leasing, exploration, and development decisions by providing timely and appropriately prepared information, and
- To monitor in order to detect changes in the quality and productivity of potentially affected environments.

As you are aware the essence of the agency mission is to manage offshore oil and gas leasing, exploration and development in an environmentally sound and safe fashion. The Environmental Studies Program seeks to support that major mission of the agency in the ways listed above and in your packets. Most importantly we are striving to obtain and move quality science in a timely and useful format and approach in to MMS decision processes.

The specific goals of this meeting are to provide an exchange of the environmental studies program in Alaska in an open forum, more particularly to provide an opportunity for priority users such as the Alaska Region's Environmental Assessment analysts and the public to refresh familiarity with the progress and results of the various studies thereby enhancing the use of the information.

We also want to share and integrate information with that of other agencies and researchers, people who know of things that are worthy of being brought in to consideration. Also, the purpose of a meeting such as this is to obtain additional public input on the plans and processes that we use and that may be useful to MMS in guiding this program.

In the past, I have used this introductory moment to talk about the various studies program accomplishments since we last met. However, that information is easily accessible in a variety of ways, so I won't dwell on it at any great length. For example, recently the Arctic Research Journal of the United States, Volume 18, Spring-Summer 2004 has seven pages that give a summary of the accomplishments of the Alaska Environmental Studies Program. We have information on our website, and, of course, the presentations at this meeting.

So I'll forego other details other than to say that the program continues to be very successful in achieving these goals by staying focused on mission, seeking to do quality and timely science, in considering and respecting local communities and their role in the studies process.

3

We also coordinate and cooperate with other research programs as much as possible, such as our recent collaborations with the National Oceanographic Partnership Program, also known as NOPP, through our cooperative agreement with the University of Alaska Fairbanks for the Coastal Marine Institute, and other interagency activities within and outside of the Department of the Interior.

We appreciate the close coordination and collaborative spirit that these contacts provide as well as our contacts with industry, with particular note of BP and ConocoPhillips who are receptive to the needs that environmental studies researchers have for access and who provide matching funds for some projects.

Currently MMS supports more than 60 ongoing Alaska OCS studies in diverse disciplines, a major portion of those are cooperatively funded. Many of these are co-funded and managed under the Coastal Marine Institute. The CMI is a multi-year cost sharing agreement designed to obtain the benefits from the University of Alaska's world-class scientific expertise. We do have a number of other interagency agreements with other research organizations offering capabilities in other needed areas.

Additional program information is available in the meeting packets. Speaking of accomplishments, please see the list of recent Alaska reports. These are the number one product that we seek to obtain and provide to the analysts who use them in their environmental assessment work. There is also a summary of the list of the ongoing studies, some information on our study planning processes, a Focus Sheet on our Environmental Studies Program. Also, there is a description of the Environmental Studies Program Information System that is a web-accessible retrieval system. You can get our reports through that system. There is also a comment form in your packet that can be used to capture your ideas about possible hypotheses we might want to test or other suggestions. Please use those and feel free to drop them off at the registration desk.

I would like to talk a little bit about our ongoing planning. First, we are in the process of, and currently working from, a *Fiscal Year 2005 Studies Plan* which is available on the Alaska Region's website. We are implementing studies that are listed there as proposed new starts. We distributed that plan to 200 important stakeholder organizations for information and comment last September. Secondly, for your information, I will be placing out on the table a list of study titles, staff contacts, and related draft study profiles for what we are calling "New Study Considerations for Fiscal Year 2006." It is a draft of concepts that we have developed to date for likely inclusion in our FY 06 Plan, which will come out next September.

Shown are the study titles and the name of the individual who is the staff scientist point-of-contact for each study concept. If you would like to discuss the motivations or the architecture for a proposed project, you need to contact those people. I would like to introduce them: Warren Horowitz should be contacted if you are interested in the first study; Dick Prentki has a number of physical oceanography studies; Kate Wedemeyer handles fisheries-type projects; which are the remaining FY 06 projects; Jeff Gleason has interest in migratory birds, and Dee Williams is our sociocultural specialist. So if you are interested in the nature of these proposed projects, those are the people you need to see.

There are a few special welcomes that I would like to mention this morning, some of whom are maybe *in absentia* since they are recovering from the celebrations of Fur Rondy and the Iditarod. For those of you who haven't met them, please take the time to speak to members of our Scientific Committee and representatives of the Arctic Subcommittee of the Scientific Committee: Dr. Michael Castellini, Dr. William Schroeder, and Dr. Lee Huskey. We especially want to welcome members of the Committee. The Committee provides our program with advice on the appropriateness and the quality of the science within the Environmental Studies Program, not only here in Alaska but also on the national level. So we thank you very much for coming.

Also, Dr. Vera Alexander is here from the Coastal Marine Institute of which she is the director. We appreciate very much the technical vision that Vera has brought to the Institute over the years. We are entering our 13th year for the CMI. Dr. Alexander's leadership has been supportive and helpful throughout those years.

We also want to welcome members of the writing team for the Arctic Council's project entitled "Assessment of the Effects of Oil and Gas Activities in the Arctic" as a part of the Arctic Assessment and

Monitoring Program or AMAP. Included are national representatives of the United States, Norway, and Canada. We wish you the best of results in your concurrent information exchange and discussions this week.

We are also glad to see our colleagues from MMS headquarters: Ron Lai, Walter Johnson, Jeff Ji, Tom Ahlfeld, Jim Bennett, and Lee Benner. It is nice to have all of you here.

I would also like to remind the principal investigators to confirm any project-specific meetings that your COTR may have proposed. There is a meeting immediately following this meeting today on Physical Oceanography integration.

Now about the meeting specifics: Each of these sessions is going to be chaired by one or more of the MMS environmental studies scientists. They can be identified with their red nametags. Feel free to ask questions of them and any of the presenters at the end of each presentation. We ask folks to be sensitive to time so that everyone has a chance to ask questions. The session chairs will be watching the time to help speakers and sessions stay on schedule.

If you have any particular needs related to the meeting, please see Kathy Mitchell with MBC Applied Environmental Sciences who is the meeting support contractor and who manages the registration desk. Tim Holder of the MMS Environmental Studies staff is also involved with the coordination of this meeting. You can bring any matters to their attention.

That concludes my remarks. Now with great pleasure I would like to introduce Mr. Paul Stang, Regional Supervisor for the Alaska Region's Office of Leasing and Environment.

ALASKA OCS REGION ACTIVITIES
AND ENVIRONMENTAL ASSESSMENT PROCESS

Paul Stang

Regional Supervisor for Leasing and Environment
MMS, Alaska OCS Region
3801 Centerpoint Drive, Anchorage, AK 99503

Good morning. It is good to see so many familiar faces here. I looked over the agenda and it looks quite interesting, a lot of good topics. I am sure with Cleve and his staff you will be in good hands. I want to thank you all for coming. The talks for this ITM are quite important to give you an overview of what MMS is doing. Not only in your particular area of interest, but that you hear each other's topics so that we have some integration. One of the key issues that the MMS Scientific Advisory Committee is concerned with is making sure that everyone is talking to everyone else--the physical oceanographers are talking to the biologists, etc. That is a key element. A lot can be gained by that type of cross-fertilization.

I would like to present an overview of the activities of the MMS Outer Continental Shelf program. Figure 1 shows the MMS OCS planning areas with which you are all familiar. We refer to the *Final Outer Continental Shelf Oil and Gas Leasing Program 2002-2007* for short as the Five-Year Program. It includes Lease Sales proposed in the: Beaufort Sea in 2003, 2005, and 2007; Cook Inlet 2004 and 2006; Chukchi Sea/Hope Basin (up to two Sales); and Norton Basin (one Sale). The later two areas are interest-based Sales with annual calls. The most important planning areas are the Beaufort Sea and Cook Inlet.

Rising in importance is the Chukchi Sea area, at least from the interest that we have been receiving. Some of the other areas are of some question. For some this will probably be the last time you will hear about them for five years.

Figure 1. MMS OSC planning areas.

What drives the interest by companies is the potential of the area. The Environmental Studies Program is shaped by the context of the areas of industry interest. One of our primary tasks is deciding which areas to offer for lease and then provide the terms, which allow that. Should there be exploration and successful development, then allow it to go forward in an environmentally sound manner. That is the focus.

To have a lease sale we need to have adequate environmental information. Typically, the environmental information is a significant component of an environmental impact statement (EIS) or environmental assessment (EA). To prepare and EIS or EA, we need environmental information that you, the scientists and experts, produce.

So where is our current the focus? For the Chukchi Sea and Beaufort Sea, there is good potential, see Table 1. Hope Basin, at least in the optimistic scenario for gas looks pretty good as does the Norton Basin area. Remember those are the optimistic scenarios. The other side of those two doesn't look so optimistic here.

Table 1. Alaska OCS Hydrocarbon Potential for 2002-2007 Five-Year Program Areas. (Risked, undiscovered, conventionally recoverable) Low to High Estimates (MMS 2000 National Assessment).

Planning Area	Oil (billions barrels)	Gas (trillion cubic feet)
Alaska OCS Total	*17-35*	*55-227*
Chukchi Sea	9-25	14-154
Beaufort Sea	4-12	13-63
Hope Basin	0-0.3	0-11
Norton Basin	0-0.2	0-9
Cook Inlet	0.3-1.4	0.7-2.5

So that is a good perspective to keep in mind as we look at areas in the future.

We are a little more than half way through the current Five-Year Program that ends in June of 2007. In that program we have what are called "traditional sale areas" in the Beaufort Sea and Cook Inlet. In Beaufort Sea and Cook Inlet there has been exploration and development. The development in Cook Inlet has not been in federal waters but in nearby state waters. Of course, in the Beaufort, most of the development is onshore and in state waters with a little in federal waters. So those are the areas where we have held traditional sales that are ones where you go through a very rigorous process with an EIS, etc.

In more speculative areas where there has not been production, interest tends not to be as strong. We have developed area interest-based sales. MMS does this in a way not to make a big commitment of staff resources to an area that has a low probability of industry interest. So a call for interest and information is issued. If no one comes forward, we just stop. We then wait another year and issue another call. In the current Five-Year Program for the Chukchi Sea we have a limit of two Sales using that process; in Norton Basin, a limit of one sale. By following this procedure, staff resources are not wasted going through a substantial environmental analysis for an area in which industry is not interested.

MMS has Beaufort Sea Sale 195 scheduled for March 30, 2005. We did a multiple-sale EIS for the three Sales we have scheduled for the Beaufort Sea. The Beaufort Sea Program Area is illustrated in Figure 2. We tiered off of the multiple-sale EIS with an EA which is much shorter. MMS finished and issued the EA and public comment was received. I think that process worked quite well. We received comments from the North Slope Borough, the Alaska Eskimo Whaling Commission, and Earth Justice. We also received a number of public comments.

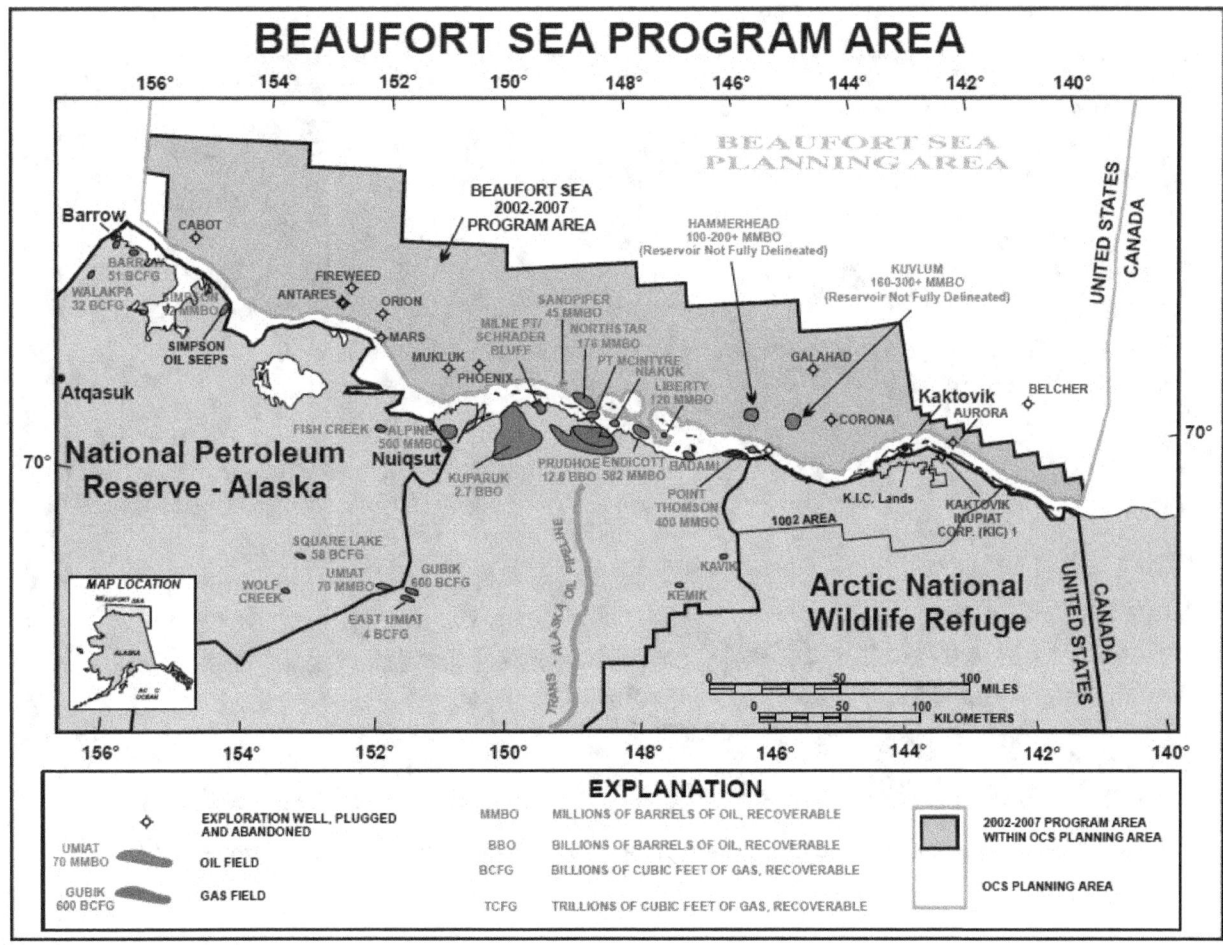

Figure 2. Beaufort Sea oil and gas leasing activity.

[Post script: At the Sale on March 30 oil companies spent $46.7 million on winning bids on 127 blocks. Of the total, Shell accounted for $44.4 million in bids on 86 blocks. Shell showed the most interest in a discovery known as Hammerhead 60 miles east of Prudhoe Bay.]

An unexpected outcome of this process was that the State determined that a separate consistency review was not required for this subsequent Sale. The State felt that the one consistency review at the multiple Sale stage, when we first issued it, would be sufficient.

MMS has had ongoing dialogue with the North Slope Borough, the Alaska Eskimo Whaling Commission and the Iñupiat Community of the Arctic Slope for years, starting rather intensively in July 2003. So we have had a series of discussions and letters about some of the areas of importance to these three organizations. This series of discussions has been fairly productive. We have made a number of commitments to things that we would do to meet some of the requirements that they have. I don't think that we have gone as far as they would like. But I think that we have gone fairly far and tried to make our process more responsive to the needs that they have expressed.

Looking more closely at the Beaufort Sea, of course, most of the action historically has been on shore and some in nearby waters. As far as MMS is concerned, the two projects of most worth are the Northstar, which is the first and only area of production in Federal waters, and Liberty.

Even though Northstar Island is in State waters, there are three down-hole locations in Federal waters. The wells are drilled directionally across the Federal-State boundary into the Federal OCS. MMS has been leasing since 1979 and gathering a lot of money from industry in these Lease Sales, but so far the only production has been the three down hole locations in Northstar. Figure 3 shows a photograph of Northstar development just prior to production start in 2001. The Northstar location, illustrated in Figure 4, is just south of the Federal-State boundary.

Figure 3. Northstar Island, looking north, September 2001. Production began in November 2001.

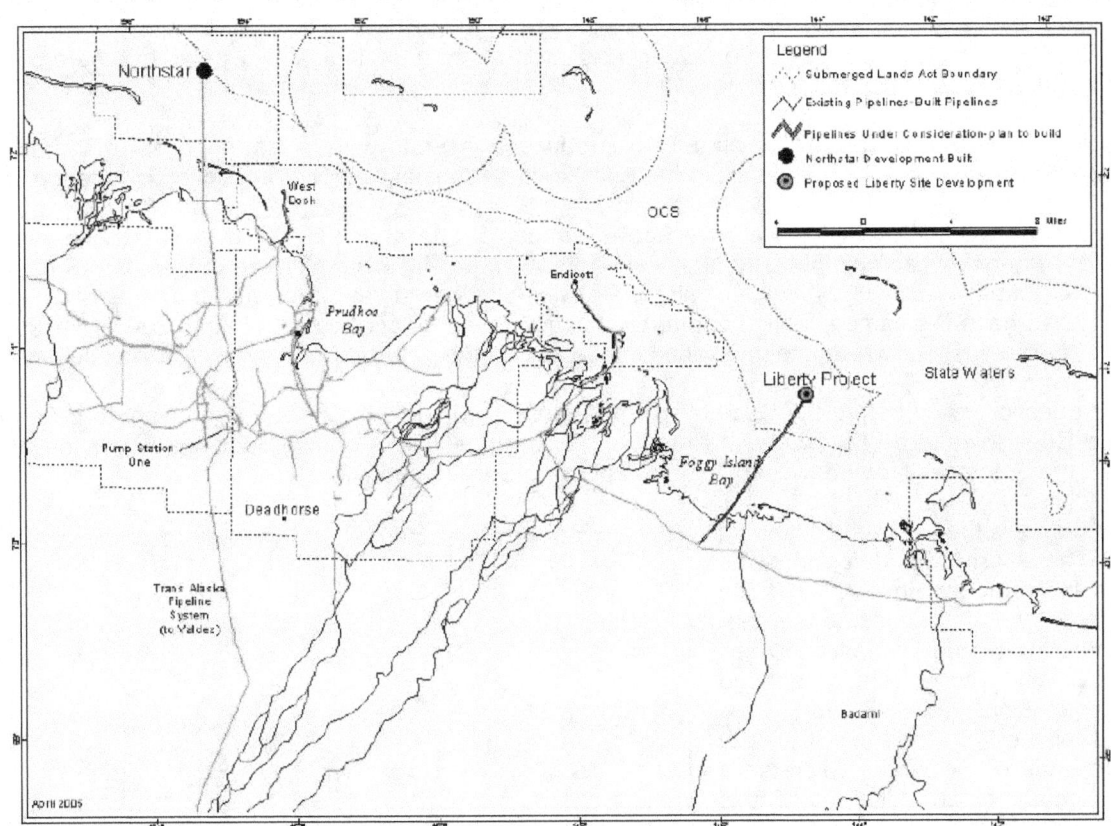

Figure 4. Northstar and Liberty development areas.

BP submitted the Liberty development and production plan in 1998. In 2002 MMS completed the EIS and BP decided to hold off and rethink development of the Liberty prospect. That is what BP has been doing since then. This year they have indicated an interest in coming in with a new development and production plan in about June 2006. The Liberty development site and one of the pipeline routes considered for development are illustrated in Figure 4.

For Northstar, one of the most interesting things is the pipeline that comes all the way into shore and then to existing pipelines. The Liberty development and production plan of 1998 had two options: a pipeline that came straight to shore and one coming to shore in a southeasterly direction.

Basically, with Liberty, this issue was should you process on the island offshore or should you send the three phase product (oil, gas, and water) to shore and process it there? If it is brought to shore and processed, it would probably be at Badami or Endicott. In the next year or so we will see the answers to those questions unfold, how the products will come to shore and whether it will be a buried pipeline or an elevated one.

Earlier I mentioned the "special interest sales" for the Chukchi Sea, and Hope and Norton Basin. We have annual calls for interest. We have had three such calls. The last one closes in May. It will be interesting to see if industry is interested in Chukchi. Some companies have expressed some interest but we'll see if they will follow through with actual leasing.

These are frontier areas without production. A requirement of the special interest sales is a commitment to drill by the eighth year. If they don't then they lose the lease. So if someone is interested, MMS wants them to go ahead and explore. Industry leased some tracts in the Chukchi Sea over 25 years ago.

Industry did find some real evidence of gas there. But that is a pretty remote location and the economics weren't there to proceed. The price of gas and oil has gone substantially higher since that time.

In the Norton Basin, the prospects aren't nearly as strong from a geological viewpoint, but there certainly is local interest in use of gas there.

In Cook Inlet there has been a fair amount of production in State waters that supplies Anchorage and other communities and some industries in the Nikiski area also with gas. But production is tapering off.

In Federal waters in Cook Inlet, we have had a number of Lease Sales. There have been a variety of levels of controversy, some higher, some lower at other times. MMS completed a multi-sale EIS for Lease Sales 191 and 199 in 2003. MMS had Sale 191 a little less than a year ago and no company expressed interest. We have the same situation confronting us for Sale 199 scheduled for April 2006. We issued a call for that Sale. There was some opposition expressed by the public, but no industry expressed interest.

So the question really before the Secretary of the Interior right now is "What do you want to do with this second Cook Inlet Sale? Do you want to delay it?" That question is pending and we'll hear the answer soon. If the Sale goes forward, we would tier off of the EIS using an EA.

Figure 5 shows the Cook Inlet planning area. There are two deferral areas shown in green and in purple. Those deferrals were requested rather strongly by a number of Native villages in the vicinity. Those were considered in the multiple-sale EIS and were picked for the first Cook Inlet Sale. Of course, that is part of the Secretary's job to make those decisions if this subsequent Sale 199 goes forward.

The current Five-Year program ends in June 2007. Quite frankly, we thought that we would have the Federal Register notice out by the end of December announcing the new Five-Year program. There is a rather elaborate process that is outlined in the OCS Lands Act in Section 18. So you have to start a couple of years ahead. The people at headquarters of MMS and in the Department are still thinking about that and working on it. What kind of initial notice they would like to have, etc. So hopefully, fairly soon we'll see that come. Then that process will start. It is very familiar to those who have been through it. We have several versions and an EIS that goes with those documents.

The driving force of the program is the resources and, therefore, how much industry interest might there be. That is a key element driven to a large degree not by current prices, but the expectation of future prices. The companies have to figure out what the

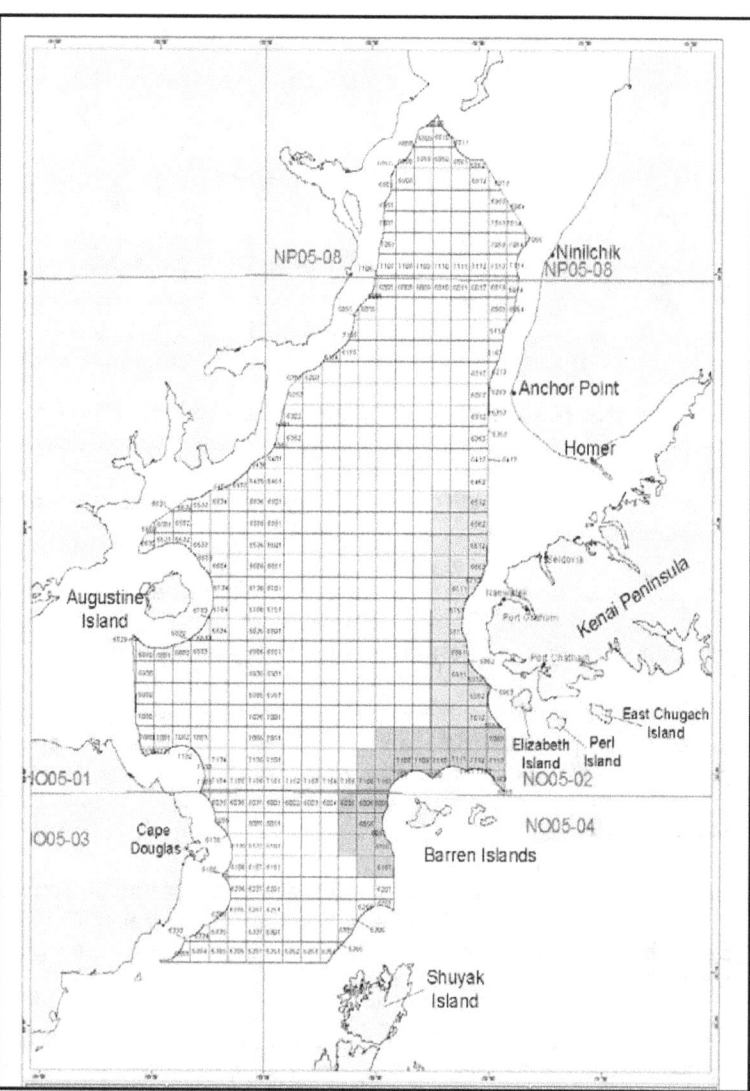

Figure 5. Cook Inlet Planning Area and Deferral Areas.

price of oil is going to be in five, ten, or 15 years. How they do that, I am never quite sure. Then they can make their judgments about whether they should lease and where.

There is an estimated 191 trillion cubic feet (TCF) of gas with 82% of that in the Arctic. The Arctic portion includes 64 TCF in Northern Alaska onshore, 32 TCF in the U.S. Beaufort Sea, and 60 TCF in the U.S. Chukchi Sea.

Of course, another element is a natural gas pipeline. There have been 30 plus years of reinjected gas sitting up there in the North Slope just waiting for a pipeline. So if you are going to be producing new gas, that is you are looking today about producing gas, you have a 30 year supply just sitting there waiting to be sent down the pipeline. Whether we get one or not, is always a question. As anyone experienced in this area knows--we will know only when it happens.

In trying to look a little more broadly than just our own little world of MMS, the Bureau of Land Management (BLM) is leasing in the National Petroleum Reserve-Alaska (NPR-A). MMS has assisted BLM with the geological work, helped prepare EIS's, and helped in the leasing process. So MMS has worked in partnership with the BLM to assist them. I think at this point, they really are going to take it on their own to a large degree, especially, in the environmental and leasing areas. We are always ready to consult with them especially on the geologic work.

BLM held NPR-A Sales for the NE in May 1999, NE-2 in June 2002, and NW in June 2004. BLM is planning a Sale for NE-3 for the summer of 2005. Of course, these aren't the first Sales in NPR-A. There have been Sales years back but nothing much came of those. There has been renewed interest. There are industry representatives in the audience who can tell you far more than I know about all of this. NPR-A stretches from the Colville River and Nuiqsut on the east to the Chukchi coast on the northwest and from the Arctic Ocean on the north to the northern foothills of the Brooks Range and Colville River on the south.

The State a few years back decided to do annual area-wide Sales. The State of Alaska has held Lease Sales on its lands that are both onshore and offshore within 3 miles of the seaward boundary. The State held: North Slope Sales for the Foothills Areawide in May 2004 and Areawide in October 2004; Beaufort Sea Sale Areawide in October 2004; and Cook Inlet Sale Areawide in May 2004. The State plans to hold an Alaska Peninsula Sale Areawide in October 2005 or sometime thereafter.

Again welcome. I hope this meeting goes well. I know you are in good hands with Cleve and his staff. Thank you very much.

Physical Oceanography

WATER AND ICE DYNAMICS OF COOK INLET

Mark Johnson[1], Ph.D., Andrey Proshutinsky[2], Ph.D., and Steve Okkonen[1,3]

[1]Institute of Marine Sciences, University of Alaska Fairbanks
Fairbanks, AK 99775, (907) 474-6933, Email: ffjfm@uaf.edu
[2]Dept. of Physical Oceanography, Woods Hole Oceanographic Institution,
Woods Hole, MA 02543, (508) 289-2796, Email: aproshutinsky@whoi.edu
[3] (907) 283-3234, Fax (907) 283-3234, E-mail: okkonen@alaska.net

We have used a 3-D tidal model (Finite Volume Community Model – FVCOM) of Cook Inlet with spatial resolution of 160 m near the coastline and 13 km along the open boundary to simulate the 8 major tidal waves in this region (5 semidiurnal and 3 diurnal). Tidal data are from satellite-based archives of tidal constituents for the Gulf of Alaska and Northern Pacific Ocean. Model results of the tidal elevations and phases of the four major waves are in good agreement with observations.

To help validate the model and understand better the Cook Inlet tidal rips, more than 25 drifting buoys have been deployed by Cook Inlet Spill Prevention and Response, Inc. (CISPRI) and others. Velocities are computed using centered differences and the processed velocity data were converted to kinetic energy. Contours of the highest energy are located east of Kalgin Island, along the middle rip. The energy contours appear to align along the steep bathymetric slope.

Fronts are typically associated with convergence zones. In Cook Inlet, drifting sea ice tends to collect along tide rip fronts thereby providing strong visual signatures for frontal locations. Radar backscatter (brightness) from sea ice is typically larger than from open water. As a consequence, the ice edge (frontal) location exhibits a relatively large spatial gradient in radar backscatter. Frontal locations identified from nine SAR images acquired in February 2002, December 2003, January 2004, and February 2004 show that the greatest number of frontal features occurs in a zone extending southwestward from near the West Foreland to along and beyond the eastern shore of Kalgin Island. This zone roughly corresponds to the location of the West Rip and qualitatively agrees with the buoy observations and model results.

Discussion:

Lie-Yauw Oey: You mentioned the Finite Volume Community Model has already been applied for wetting and drying. Have you applied it to other areas, not here?

Mark Johnson: No. We have not done the wetting and drying problem. My understanding is that the code has flags for wetting and drying. What we need to introduce are the actual boundaries of the mudflats, if you will. So once you have those data, I understand we can just turn them all on and run that.

Lie-Yauw Oey: No. I mean not this area, any other areas, to test the scheme and application of your model? Any other areas, not in Cook Inlet?

Mark Johnson: No.

Lie-Yauw Oey: So it's not used before?

Mark Johnson: I have not used it before. C. Chen of the University of Massachusetts, who developed this code, told me that the wetting and drying is in there and ready to run and it's been validated. I don't have personal knowledge of that.

Unidentified: I have two questions. One is, your model, you haven't turned on the rivers, is that correct? I just want to make sure.

Mark Johnson: Right.

Unidentified: Number two is, it is interesting that in looking at your drifter data that, it is my impression that the drifters mostly stay in that area, especially those released east of Kalgin Island. Are they mostly staying there? Over a long period of time, that's what I'm trying to say.

Mark Johnson: Yes. That's my impression, too. They seem to converge into the rips and then track there for days, if not weeks. If you put a drifter anywhere up here, it will sit there and just track back and forth. It will be constrained to the rip until the wind event comes along, and then it will change regimes. That's a reason to include winds in these models. It's a nice tidally-driven estuary until the wind blows.

OBSERVATIONS OF HYDROGRAPHY IN CENTRAL COOK INLET, ALASKA, DURING DIURNAL AND SEMIDIURNAL TIDAL CYCLES
AND
PHYSICAL MEASUREMENTS AND SEASONAL BOUNDARY CONDITIONS IN COOK INLET, ALASKA

Stephen Okkonen, Ph.D.

Institute of Marine Science
University of Alaska Fairbanks
Box 1025, Kasilof, AK 99610
(907) 283-3234, Fax (907) 283-3234, E-mail: okkonen@alaska.net

---

Dr. Okkonen was unable to attend. His talk was presented by Dr. Mark Johnson.

Surface-to-bottom measurements of temperature, salinity, and transmissivity, as well as measurements of surface currents (vessel drift speeds) were acquired along an east-west section in central Cook Inlet, Alaska during a 26-hour period on 9-10 August 2003. These measurements are used to describe the variability of frontal features (tide rips), surface currents, and physical properties along this section during semidiurnal and diurnal tidal cycles. The amplitudes of surface tidal currents are observed to be proportional to water depth, that is, faster currents occur where the channel is deeper and slower currents occur where the channel is shallower. It directly follows that laterally sheared currents occur over bathymetric slopes. Convergence zones (fronts) are also observed to occur over bathymetric slopes. The positions and strengths of these fronts vary with the semidiurnal tide. The presence of freshwater promotes density-driven currents that alter the phase and duration of tidal currents across the section. Where mean density-driven flow is northward (along the eastern shore and near Kalgin Island), the onset of northward tidal flow (flood tide) occurs earlier and has longer duration than the onset and duration of northward tidal flow where mean density-driven flow is southward (in the shipping channel). Conversely, where mean density-driven flow is southward (in the shipping channel), the onset of southward tidal flow (ebb tide) occurs earlier and has longer duration than the onset and duration of southward tidal flow along the eastern shore and near Kalgin Island. Qualitative comparisons of bathymetry and proximity to freshwater sources are used to infer characteristics of frontal features and surface currents at other locations in Cook Inlet.

Discussion:

Unidentified: Has anyone done any ADCP surveys of this whole area?

Mark Johnson: Yes. I have done some ADCP surveys. The most interesting thing that they show is the vertical velocity that you get from the ADCP shows that in the convergence zones, on an ebb tide, there is measurable downward vertical velocity that comes back to the surface 5 to 6 kilometers away. It is like an internal deformation radius away. Then it comes to the surface so you get these vertical circulation cells on top of the northward and southward structure that the previous two talks have focused on.

Michael Castellini: Mark, you made the point that the first drogues were set in 5 to 10 meters. Is anybody working on the top meter, the areas that we are concerned about the oil flowing?

Mark Johnson: That's not something that we're doing. My answer to that is that by validating the model with tracking the 5 to 10 meter layer fluid you can test whether the model is working well. Then if you now force a wind on that you can start to get the surface layer. Sue Saupe, who is director of the Cook Inlet Regional Citizens Advisory Council, has in-kind support for this project and she buys our drifters. And I think what I'm going to have her do is also buy, on top of what we have been budgeted, a few that are undrogued and put them over by Drift River and just see where they go. And that will be just a little bonus effort to address specifically that question.

HIGH RESOLUTION NUMERICAL MODELING OF NEAR-SURFACE WEATHER CONDITIONS OVER COOK INLET AND SHELIKOF STRAIT

Peter Q. Olsson, Ph.D. and Haibo Liu, Ph.D.

Alaska Experimental Forecast Facility
University of Alaska Anchorage
2811 Merrill Field Drive, Anchorage, AK 99501
(907) 264-7449, Fax (907) 264-7444, Email: olsson@aeff.uaa.alaska.edu

---

It is common knowledge to mariners in Alaska's Cook Inlet and Shelikof Strait (CISS) that there exist small (mesoscale) wind and weather regimes that are not at all indicative of the large scale conditions over the area. Indeed the near-surface winds can vary by 90 degrees or more from synoptic flow in direction and be much stronger than would be suggested by large-scale pressure gradients. However, the relative paucity of direct wind observations in this sparsely-settled region makes quantification of these mesoscale phenomena unfeasible, however apparent they are to mariners and aviators traversing the region at any given time.

The purpose of this project is to aid the understanding of these various wind regimes by using a high-resolution numerical model of the atmosphere to simulate the three-dimensional weather in the region of interest at a scale much smaller than that of current operational weather forecasting models. The results of these simulations can then be used to quantify in detail the relative frequency of occurrence of these small scale ($O[10$ km$]$) weather features, their duration, and the details of their horizontal and vertical structure.

At the Alaska Experimental Forecast Facility (AEFF) we have been running the Regional Atmospheric Modeling System (RAMS) in a multiply-nested forecast mode for the CISS region using a grid mesh of 4 km spacing. The model is run daily and is initialized using NCEP Eta model initial fields and forecasts for initial and lateral boundary conditions respectively. The model is initialized at 00 UTC and integrated forward for 36 hours with data writes occurring every hour. The model results are posted in graphical form on the AEFF Weather Briefer's Page:

http://aeff.uaa.alaska.edu/wx_brief.html

and the various numerical fields are archived for future use by the AEFF and others interested in CISS weather conditions.

This nested grid approach allows us to simulate the interaction of the large scale weather systems ($O[1000$ km$]$ with the extreme terrain variations of the CISS region that can vary dramatically on the scale $O[1$ km$]$. The results reveal a variety of ageostrophic channeled and gap flows that have time scales

17

ranging from a few hours to several days and spatial scales varying from several kilometers to the full extent of Cook Inlet and the Shelikof Strait. Comparisons with satellite-borne Synthetic Aperture Radar (SAR) wind speed retrievals shows that RAMS has the capability to faithfully reproduce several of the wind features seen in the SAR images.

Discussion:

Lie-Yauw Oey: I have many questions. But just to start with this one, is the data available on your website?

Peter Olsson: The graphics are available on the website. The actual numbers are not. You need to make special arrangements.

Lie-Yauw Oey: Now, I'm curious about something. Those jets that you showed, are those topographically driven? Like the Turnagain Arm jet?

Peter Olsson: Yes. The Turnagain Arm jet is definitely topographically driven. If you took all the topography away, which you can do with the model, you still see, because of the pressure gradient configuration, areas of high wind and areas of low wind, but they're not confined to the various channels like they are in the views that I showed you.

Lie-Yauw Oey: The satellite data, the SAR data you showed, are those SSMI satellite data?

Peter Olsson: No, it is Canadian SAR-SAT.

Leo Oey: And they have no problem close to the coast?

Peter Olsson: They have problems very close to the coast, but they do a pretty good job. They're at about a 400-meter resolution.

Lie-Yauw Oey: No. What I'm talking about is the interference with the land and all that. If I understand it, SSMI has a limit of 25 kilometers.

Peter Olsson: No. I mean the images are definitely degraded for the obvious reasons close to the coastline. But given the small pixel size, they are pretty good once you get a few kilometers away from the coastline. I can't tell you exactly, the exact number, but it's nothing like QuickSCAT winds.

Lie-Yauw Oey: That's my next question. Did you check with QuickSCAT?

Peter Olsson: We haven't done any comparisons with QuickSCAT yet on this project.

Jeff Ji: I have a quick question about the cluster of computer you use. Here you have like a 27 CPU, is that right?

Peter Olsson: That's right.

Jeff Ji: How much you speed up the model by using the clustered computers?

Peter Olsson: I would say on the 27 nodes we probably get about 16 times speed-up over a single node.

Jeff Ji: And do you need to do a special treatment to your code to make it use the multiple node processes?

Peter Olsson: I didn't do it. The RAMs code is available through the new public license, GPL. It already has the parallel processing, the MPI code, built into it. So that's not something that we did specially ourselves. We didn't parallelize the existing code. We took code that already had parallelization in it. But of course there's a big step from getting the code to getting it to run the way you want it to.

SEA ICE MODELING FOR BEAUFORT AND CHUKCHI SEAS

Matthew Pruis[1], Max Coon[1], Ron Kwok[2], Deborah Sulsky[3], Buck Schreyer[3] and Leif Toudal[4]

[1] NorthWest Research Associates, 14508 NE 20th Street, Bellevue, WA 98007
(425) 644-9660, Fax (425) 644-8422, E-mail: matt@nwra.com
[2] Jet Propulsion Laboratory, California Institute of Technology,
4800 Oak Grove Drive, Pasadena, CA 91109
(818) 354-5614, Fax (818) 393-3077, E-mail: ron.kwok@jpl.nasa.gov
[3] University of New Mexico, Department of Mathematics and Statistics and the Department of Mechanical Engineering, Albuquerque, New Mexico, 87131
(505) 277-7425, Fax (505) 277-5505, E-mail: sulsky@math.unm.edu
[4] Technical University of Denmark, Øersted·DTU
Building 348, Øersted Plads, Lyngby, Denmark DK-2800
45 45 25 3791, Fax 45 45 93 1634, E-mail: ltp@oersted.dtu.dk

Dr. Pruis was unable to attend the meeting but we provide this summary because it is for an ongoing study.

The objectives of this program are to implement, test, and validate a new sea ice dynamics model that will treat the pack as elastic ice regions of ice that are delineated by regions of motion discontinuities, and incorporate the correct frazil/pancake behavior in the marginal ice zone. We have developed a discrete constitutive equation for predicting the initiation and evolution of motion discontinuities in Arctic pack ice. Important features of the model are the ability to describe the direction(s), amount of opening across, and shear along the discontinuities. The discontinuities may represent a single lead or sets of leads that explain the divergence, compaction and shear of a region of ice. In the marginal ice zone, we are developing an ice model in which new ice grows as frazil and pancake ice instead of sheet ice growth. This is important along an advancing / freezing ice edge. Air temperatures along the ice edge are usually moderated by the open water—a process that slows the growth of sheet ice. Substantial volumes of ice can still be grown at these moderate air temperatures however, if the ice grows as frazil and pancake ice. Ice production has a large effect on the rate of expansion of the first-year ice.

The pack ice model is based on an elastic-decohesion formulation. Thus far we have not included plasticity in the model formulation. Unique aspects of this model are the ability to predict axial splitting under uniaxial compression, to handle multiple discontinuities at a point, to predict modes of failure according to the state of stress, and to incorporate pre-existing planes of weakness. Simulations have been performed for a 250 square kilometer region in the Beaufort Sea, and compared with ice motion data obtained from satellite-derived synthetic aperture radar. The frazil / pancake marginal ice zone model has been formulated and validated by assimilating passive microwave data obtained from satellites.

SEA *ICE-OCEAN*-OILSPILL MODELING *S*YSTEM (*SIOMS*) FOR THE NEARSHORE BEAUFORT AND CHUKCHI SEAS: IMPROVEMENT AND PARAMETERIZATION (PHASE II)

Jia Wang, Meibing Jin, and Sheng Zhang

International Arctic Research Center, University of Alaska Fairbanks
Fairbanks, AK 99775-7335. (907) 474-2685, Fax (907) 474-2643, Email: jwang@iarc.uaf.edu

This three-year continued project aims at improving the existing high-resolution coupled ice-ocean model using available observations and at investigating the fine structure of the ice and ocean circulation. The improvements include 1) the Bering Strait opening that allows ~1 Sv throughflow into the Chukchi Sea, 2) the extended nested boundary that is further from the nearshore Beaufort and Chukchi Seas, and 3) the extended minimum depth from 10 m to 5 m. A parameterization of longwave radiation (Zillman 1972) is added to improve the heat balance of the sea ice. The improved model was implemented in supercomputers at the Alaska Region Supercomputing Center (ARSC). The modeling results will be demonstrated.

To validate the model, we focus on a systematic model-data comparison. We are now processing Japan Marine Science and Technology Center - JAMSTEC (matching funds) moored ADCP data in the Beaufort Sea for the period from 1990-2000. Sixteen moored ADCPs have been collected, which allocated at depths from 50 m to 200 m, and each spanning about one year. We have processed the data at several stations. The results indicate 1) on the shelfbreak (less than 200 m), there is a persistent eastward flow in the Beaufort Sea with average speed of 20 cm/s, 2) vertical structure of the eastward current tends to be unstable due to unstable water column because the vertical shear is small, and 3) tidal current is weak. The spectral analysis shows that strong variability occurs at time scales of about 10 days and 3-4 days, indicating synoptic weather system contributes to the variations. The monthly mean circulation patterns at different depths will be constructed based on the 16 moorings, which will be compared with our improved version of the model.

Literature Cited:

Zillman, J.W. 1972. Isentropically time-averaged mass circulation in the Southern Hemisphere. Ph.D. Thesis, University of Wisconsin-Madison. 205 p.

Discussion:

Lie-Yauw Oey: Can you just briefly describe JAMSTEC measurements and how you actually did all that stuff?

Jia Wang: JAMSTEC they visit here every year, almost every year. They deploy and retrieve moorings. Usually every year they put in two or three moorings. Because the International Arctic Research Center is sponsored by JAMSTEC, we collaborate and have access to their data.

Lie-Yauw Oey: Other people can't use their data?

Jia Wang: Even I cannot use the data without permission. I can use the data for data-model comparison. I cannot use the data itself.

SIMULATION OF LANDFAST SEA ICE ALONG THE ALASKAN COAST

Mark Hopkins, Ph.D.

Cold Regions Research Environmental Laboratory, U.S. Army Corps of Engineers
72 Lyme Rd., Hanover, NH 03755
(603) 646-4249, Email: Mark.A.Hopkins@erdc.usace.army.mil

The northern Alaska coastline is a region where the native Inuit population, non-native residents, marine and terrestrial ecosystems are intimately connected to seasonal changes in the frozen landscape. The traditional patterns of subsistence hunting, fishing, and whaling for the Inuit are tied to the cycle of growth and retreat of the land fast sea ice. The migration of bowhead whales through coastal waters follows the spring opening of the ice cover and the associated surge of biological activity. The opening of the ice cover increases risks of coastal travel. Events such as *ivu*, when sea ice is driven onto the land, can also be hazardous to coastal villages. Northern Alaska's non-subsistence economy, driven in part by oil and gas resource development and extraction from Prudhoe Bay and gas wells in the North Slope, is constrained by the cycles of coastal sea ice. These activities provide revenue to the native corporations in oil and gas leases, in addition to employment in these fields and associated economic activity. Access to these regions by ship is constrained to the period of ice-free conditions off the coast. Delivery into Barrow and other coastal communities of many products, including vehicles, snowmobiles, construction materials, and packaged food, is accomplished by ship transport in the ice-free summer. To aid in the prediction of the growth and movement of landfast ice and coastal sea ice it would be valuable to have a sea ice model that was capable of explicitly resolving ice processes in the coastal zone including the growth and grounding of landfast ice, the growth of shore leads, and the near-shore ice motion. The goal of this project is to construct such a model.

At the Cold Regions Research and Engineering Lab (CRREL) we have constructed a high-resolution Lagrangian sea ice model of the Arctic basin that can simulate the motion of individual ice parcels, the freezing and fracturing of plates, the opening and closing of leads, and the creation of pressure ridges. The model consists of many thousands of individual floes that can freeze together. The fracture pattern created by wind-driven deformation defines a plate structure in the model ice pack. When plates separate they form leads and when pushed together they form pressure ridges. Pressure ridging is incorporated via a parameterization based on discrete element simulations of the ridging process. New ice is grown in open leads. Thermodynamic ice growth and melt are modeled using multiple thickness categories each having its own vertical temperature profile. Wind stress, water currents, temperature fields, and Coriolis accelerations drive the model pack. To model the seasonal growth and recession of landfast sea ice and coastal ice motion along the north coast of Alaska we are

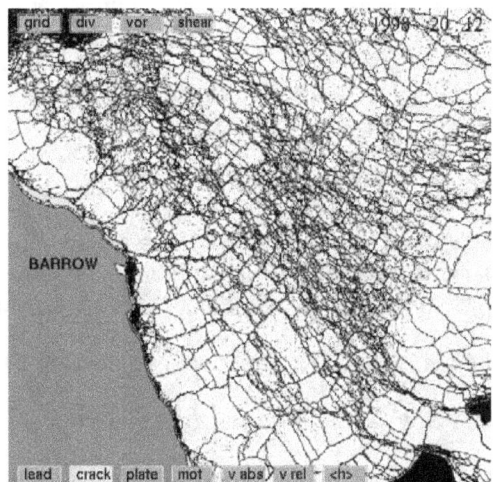

Figure showing the crack pattern and plates produced by fracture in the model pack.

extending this basin scale model in the following ways. We have constructed a 50 m resolution data set of the coastline from west of Barrow to east of Prudhoe Bay that resolves barrier islands, inlets, and oil production facilities. We are increasing the model resolution in the coastal zone to 500 m at the shore decreasing smoothly with distance from the coast to 20 km resolution at a distance of 300 km from the coast. The same 20 km resolution is used over the central basin. We are adapting the results of explicit simulations of the pressure ridging process to parameterize the growth of grounded and ungrounded coastal ice pile-up processes. These parameterizations will be used in conjunction with coastal bathymetry to explicitly model pile-up and grounding of ice along the north Alaskan coast. Finally, we will adapt the ice model to use high-resolution coastal currents to capture detailed current driven ice motion.

Discussion:

Lie-Yauw Oey: How thick was the ice?

Mark Hopkins: Again, this is not starting with a realistic distribution. This is something like two meters, initially, but then the thin ice that's being created is ..., begins with open water. These big flaw leads, there's open water. So that black represents very thin ice that's being transported up in here.

Lie-Yauw Oey: So the time scale for break-up is 40 days?

Mark Hopkins: No. This is just an on-going process. The variation is just your synoptic scale weather forcing every few days. You're just seeing synoptic weather patterns going back, and coming through.

Tom Newbury: None of your simulations reproduce the very persistent lead that develops from Barrow going east offshore. It must be that the ice against the coast is more fixed there. At any rate, there's a very persistent lead that develops each year, going east from Barrow that the bowhead whales follow when they migrate north and east. In the simulation that you just showed, it shows all of the ice moving west. And it must be that the nearshore ice is fixed somehow because year after year there's a lead that develops going from Barrow east over toward Canada. So it must be that that nearshore ice is fixed somehow, that it shears out there.

Mark Hopkins: I agree. I think that that's probably the definition of the landfast ice we're trying to capture here, that ice that is fixed.

Dong Ping Wang: Can you actually verify or see what the real ice should actually look like? We know nothing about this whole field. Can you image the real world or some kind of way to see what all this ...

Mark Hopkins: Yes. Out in the central pack, some folks at JPL and the Alaska SAR facility have come up with five or six years of data on motion in the central pack from the Radarsat imagery. But that's the central basin motion. More related to this study are the landfast processes that Hajo Eicken at the University of Alaska is working on. He is doing the same thing for the landfast ice zone from west of Barrow almost to the Mackenzie River. And so that's really what we're going to be comparing over the next years. He's coming up with ice motion, very detailed ice motion for that region. And he's going to talk about that later.

Lie-Yauw Oey: This is very interesting. The first question I asked was about the time scale. Now, I was thinking about, what if you have a uniform coastline, in other words, a straight coastline, filled with ice, uniform thickness, two meters thick, and you blow a wind with shear. How long before the ice breaks up?

Mark Hopkins: That just depends how much wind fetch you've got.

Lie-Yauw Oey: What about coming from –

Mark Hopkins: It would happen fast, like within 24 hours.

Lie-Yauw Oey: A few days?

Mark Hopkins: No, less than that. You can get the whole basin into a steady state in about two hours.

Lie-Yauw Oey: So this is just due to the pure wind shear?

Mark Hopkins: Yes.

Lie-Yauw Oey: And one more question, you mentioned at the beginning of the talk, your model is different from Hibler's model?

Mark Hopkins: Right. That's a continuum.

Lie-Yauw Oey: Yours is primitive?

Mark Hopkins: Right. It's primitive.

Lie-Yauw Oey: What is the difference then?

Mark Hopkins: Well, Hibler's is a continuum model that depends on a yield surface, so it kind of averages the ridging and lead-opening behavior into a plastic yield surface. My approach is to solve the discontinuum equations and use Newton's Law.

Andy Mahoney: You showed a picture where you had a distribution of points you initialized from, and there was a gradient down from a very high concentration at the coast offshore. Well, it seems that you might want a very high gradient or a very high concentration at the landfast ice edge too. And I think from your picture it looked like that was really where the landfast ice edge is, that is where your concentration dropped off. So you might to extend that out.

Mark Hopkins: It dropped off, but it was still about a kilometer.

Andy Mahoney: So, a lot better than anything else.

Mark Hopkins: Yes, that's a good point. I mean, I was going at this from kind of a blank slate, so I figured, well, we'll go from the shore out. But I think you're right. It would be better to go from the landfast ice edge out. Of course, you don't know where that is.

Andy Mahoney: In your timeline for research, you showed that you aren't going to include grounding in your model until later on. So what was holding the ice to the coast in that little animation you just showed at the end? You had landfast ice there.

Mark Hopkins: The ice was frozen to the coast, but it's not grounded.

Andy Mahoney: You have bottom-fast ice in the model?

Mark Hopkins:....the coastline, a bunch of coastline elements, that define the coastline, and then there's ice that adjacent to that that's, initially the whole thing's frozen. So when you turn the wind on, the band next to the coast stays frozen to the coast, and some distance from the coast you get the fracture forming, or the lead forming, that you alluded to. So even though it's not grounded, it's frozen to the coast.

Meibing Jin: I want to ask about how many properties do you define for each ice floe, i.e., the shape, etc.? Do you increase or change the number of floes during your model run?

Mark Hopkins: Yes. I didn't get into some of the details. Because it's a Lagrangian model, you have an explicit lead, and that lead may be 10 or 20 kilometers wide at the coast, a very wide lead. So in order to grow ice in that lead, you need to reinitialize the model, kind of reseed the model, so that you now have a continuous distribution of these things over that lead and over the rest of the basin. So there's a reinitialization that I didn't talk about. It reinitializes once a day, time steps on the order of, in this model, about a tenth of a second.

Meibing Jin: Okay. For the ice floe, does every ice floe have a shape?

Mark Hopkins: Every ice floe has a shape, a velocity, and a thickness distribution, whatever property you need to characterize it. Sorry, I didn't go into the thermodynamics. There's a thickness distribution, and then each thickness in the floe has a vertical temperature distribution in order to grow ice and melt ice.

Meibing Jin: So when you are doing the ranging, do you also change the shape?

Mark Hopkins: No. I don't. You could do that in principle, but it would add a little bit of a burden to your computation. Since I'm reinitializing daily, I'm not losing too much by not changing the shape.

23

Meibing Jin: You have ridging. You have ice floes, like piling up? And so you reinitialize those so everything has changed?

Mark Hopkins: Well, the ridging, when two polygons overlap, the ice in the overlap, the intersection, is destroyed. That gets passed to the thickness distributions of the.... I guess we can talk about it later.

DEVELOPMENT AND TESTING OF AN OCEAN MODEL WITH WETTING AND DRYING CAPABILITY FOR TIDAL AREAS [COOK INLET]

Lie-Yauw Oey, Ph.D., and Tal Ezer

AOS Program, Princeton University, Princeton, New Jersey 08544
(609) 258-5971, Fax (609) 258-2850, Email:lyo@aos.Princeton.edu

---

A three-dimensional model with wetting and drying (WAD) capability has been developed and tested for the Cook Inlet. The ocean model is based on the Princeton Regional Ocean Forecast System (PROFS) version of the Princeton Ocean Model (POM), and the WAD scheme was previously developed in Oey 2005. Here we will present some idealized model results that test the WAD scheme, then some model applications to the Cook Inlet forced by M2 tide. We show that with bottom friction values commonly used in coastal tidal models, the shallow-water system may be cast into a Burger's type equation for the total depth D. For flows dominated by D (i.e., |grad(D)| >> |grad(H)|, where H(x,y) defines topography) a nonlinear diffusion equation results, with an effective diffusivity varying as D^2, so that `dry' cells are regions where 'diffusion' is very small. In this case, the system admits D = 0 as part of its continuous solution and no checks are necessary. For general topography, and/or in the case of strong momentum advection, 'wave-breaking' solution (i.e., hydraulic jumps and/or bores) can develop. These considerations allow a simple WAD scheme in which `dry' cells are defined as regions with a thin film of fluid O (cm). The primitive equations are solved in the thin film as well as in other regular wet cells. The scheme requires only flux-blocking conditions across cells' interfaces when wet cells become dry, while 'dry' cells are temporarily dormant and are dynamically activated through mass and momentum conservation. The scheme is verified against the above-mentioned diffusion and Burger's type equations, and tested also for one and two-dimensional channel flows that contain hydraulic jumps, including a laboratory dam-break problem. The scheme is then tested for the Cook Inlet. In particular, the model simulates the flooding and drying of the Knik and Turnagin Arms. During ebb, extensive mud regions are simulated especially in the Turnagin Arm.

Literature Cited:

Oey, L.-Y. 2005. A wetting and drying scheme for the Princeton Ocean Model. Ocean Modeling 9(2): 133-150.

Discussion:

Jia Wang: For the rip tides, is that tidal average?

Lie-Yauw Oey: No. You cannot do that because the rip tide, as I understand it anyway, is transient. It disappears during slack waters. So it's only during the high tides and the ebbing tides, the strongest part of the tides, probably right up to the high tide, right up to the ebbing, the strongest ebbing, where it is formed. And it's formed due to the convergence of the waters. You cannot tidally average. You could see something tidally averaged, but it's not rip tide. The rip tide is this circulating cell that we talk about.

Frank Bercha: How do you integrate the temperature and relative density effects into the model? The thermodynamics, in other words, and the relative density? What caused me to ask it is I noticed the fresh water, in your cross sections, was down low. Of course, it is lighter than the saline water unless it's temperature compensated, so I'm just curious about that.

Lie-Yauw Oey: I did not show any temperature. But we solve temperature and salinity like a Tracer Equation. With thermodynamics, of course, it's connected to the density equation. I didn't pay too much attention to temperature, because the whole circulation is governed by salinity, most of it anyway. But we do put in the climatology, the temperature. But it could be important in summer time when you have heating, when the near-surface layers become very stratified. And that one we did not do.

Frank Bercha: I presume, therefore, that the fresh water is colder than the saline water, and that's why it sinks down? Or is that the dynamic phenomenon, because it is obviously lighter?

Lie-Yauw Oey: Did it show that?

Frank Bercha: Yes. It was down. Some of the fresh water on your cross sections was down low.

Leo Oey: You mean the cell limit?

Frank Bercha: Yes.

Lie-Yauw Oey: That salty water is actually the intrusion from the open ocean. That dominates it all. There's intrusion, and fresh water on the top.

Frank Bercha: And then the fresh water gets down?

Lie-Yauw Oey: Yes. You could get mixing, but it's not necessarily cold. In fact, for that region we probably set the heat flux to zero in our model here for this case we are doing.

Frank Bercha: The fresh water is probably, with the salinities you are talking about, a couple of percent lighter than the saline water, right? Assuming the gravity of the fresh water is less.

Lie-Yauw Oey: It just mixes. The way we handle it, if it brings down the lighter water, it just mixes.

Jerry McCutcheon: What is total sediment load discharged into Cook Inlet?

Lie-Yauw Oey: Oh, boy. I don't know. Good question, but I don't know.

MAPPING AND CHARACTERIZATION OF RECURRING SPRING LEADS AND LANDFAST ICE IN THE BEAUFORT AND CHUKCHI SEAS

Hajo Eicken[1], Lew Shapiro[1], Allison Gaylord Graves[2], Andy Mahoney[1], Patrick Cotter[1]

[1] Geophysical Institute, University of Alaska Fairbanks, POB 757320, Fairbanks, AK (907) 474-7280, Fax (907) 474-7290, E-mail: hajo.eicken@gi.alaska.edu
[2] Nuna Technologies, POB 1483, Homer, AK 99603, (907) 235-3476, E-mail: nunatech@usa.net

---

The aim of this project is to map and document changes in the spatial and temporal distribution of recurring lead systems and landfast ice extent off the coast of northern Alaska. We are analyzing remote sensing imagery, specifically Radarsat Synthetic Aperture Radar (SAR) and Advanced Very High Resolution Radiometer (AVHRR) data for the time period between 1993 and 2003. These datasets are compared to 1970/80s AVHRR imagery archived at the Geophysical Institute's GeoData Center. Details can be found at the project web site at mms.gina.alaska.edu.

After inspecting all available AVHRR imagery, channel 1 (visible) and channel 4 (thermal IR) scenes with comparatively low cloud cover (c. 30-40 from December through June) are geolocated and reprojected. An automated algorithm is employed to correct for regional variations in surface temperature or reflectance (incl. thin clouds/fog) and distinguish between open water/leads and ice. The resulting binary image is analyzed for the fraction of open water and the location, size and morphology of leads. Products from this analysis include processed imagery, lead grid and shape files in ArcGIS format and lead statistics. A distinct seasonal cycle in the fraction of open water and the number and morphology of leads is evident in the data. Winter months with low lead fractions contrast with increasing openings in the ice in May and June, as the lead morphology changes from linear leads to interconnected ponds between individual floes. We have identified a small number of characteristic lead patterns and associated processes and are examining whether their relative importance has changed in concert with large-scale changes in ice conditions and atmospheric circulation.

The monthly position of the seaward landfast ice edge (SLIE) is obtained from sets of three Radarsat SAR mosaics spaced roughly 10 days apart, employing a semi-automated algorithm. Data products include SLIE positions in the form of ArcGIS grid and shape files, as well as derived statistics. The monthly SLIE positions exhibit regions of high variability as well as stable nodes, where the position of the SLIE does not vary significantly during the course of winter and spring. While further work is needed to understand the formation of such nodes, they appear to correspond to grounded ice. Preliminary analysis also indicates that maximum landfast ice extent determined in the 1970s was further offshore than in recent years. Further work will have to clarify whether this reflects differences in methodology or a true environmental change.

This work is of relevance and potential utility from a number of perspectives. Lead and landfast ice data are key prerequisites for a number of different models currently operated by MMS and other agencies (e.g., oil spill risk and dispersal analysis). The statistics gleaned from the data can help in planning future efforts in the Alaska coastal and offshore environment. The data may also prove useful to state and federal agencies addressing wildlife and ecosystem management.

Discussion:

Mark Hopkins: When you showed that seasonal evolution of the leads, the number of leads, to what extent does that depend on your ability to see them? Is it "limited by area of sample"? Missing more in summer? We always used to talk about floe size; but when you really look at floes you find out they're fractal. If you keep magnifying it and magnifying it you see smaller and smaller...

Hajo Eicken: Yes. That's a good point. As I tried to point out, this data is limited by the ground-sampling interval, or the ground projected field-of-view of the AVHRR radiometer, which is 1.1 kilometers. Now, the segmentation algorithm that we apply to determine the presence of leads is such that we can detect leads down to 50% of the total area of the grid cell. So in theory, leads are linear, so you could argue that we're basically able to pick up any lead that is larger than 500 meters in width. Now, I showed a picture earlier, if you fly over this, there are plenty of smaller leads, although it depends on season actually. If you look at some of the field observations in wintertime, you find that the smaller leads actually do freeze up so rapidly that really only large-scale active leads survive. But the bottom line is, this number here is a function of your sampling interval, which in this case is half a kilometer.

Mark Hopkins: You alluded to it just now, but I wonder whether the detection, the ones you miss is uniform over the year or whether you are missing more in the summer, or early summer or late spring?

Hajo Eicken: Well, if the lead size distribution changes, and I guess that's something we know very little about, you could argue that as you go... I mean, if you look at this image on the right here, obviously you have numerous floes that are smaller than half a kilometer in size, because presumably this is a log-normal or Weibull-type of distribution, so you would argue that you're not catching ponds in between these floes. I think at least from the perspective that we're interested in, that probably is of less importance. Because the probability of finding open water within a given distance of a point that's located on ice in summer time is approaching one on scales of hundreds of meters, as you well know. So that's where this whole problem becomes kind of irrelevant. Whereas here it's different, I would argue that in wintertime .... [inaudible] ... than 500 meters, sizes of ten of meters or more, is much smaller as compared to summer time. But you would have to do a separate study to really quantify this properly.

Lie-Yauw Oey: How much of the development of your leads depends on subsurface water beneath the ice? It's a lot, right?

Hajo Eicken: Well, you may have jets near the landfast ice edge. This is overall. The tidal forcing doesn't seem to be so significant. Although there are people who have looked at radarsat-SAR data on subtidal or subinertial time scales and have found that mostly inertial motion actually, rather than tidal forcing, is responsible for some divergence, convergence, in the pack.

Lie-Yauw Oey: So the curve that you showed, like the percentage of probability where you can find leads, etc. that depends on the coastal current I guess, and what the eddy field is?

Hajo Eicken: At this time of year, if you look at some of these images, they express eddies very, very well. But I should point out from the MMS perspective; they are interested in the spring-time leads, this type of regime. I don't know what the role of the ocean is in these leads here.

Lie-Yauw Oey: That's very interesting. I was just wondering, maybe this discussion should be for Jia Wang. Has anybody used that information, lead information, to somehow assimilate into the ocean model?

Jia Wang: We put our ice model there and from this lead and then we can see from my circulation model results, there's a very strong shear around the lead there. So it must have something to do with the ocean circulation shear.

Hajo Eicken: If you were to plot the bathymetry at Barrow Canyon, it comes up right here and basically emerges somewhere here on the shelf. There's active upwelling on the landward side of Barrow Canyon. We've had thermister strings out here that record quite warm water even during the winter months.

SURFACE CIRCULATION RADAR MAPPING IN ALASKAN COASTAL WATERS: FIELD STUDY BEAUFORT SEA AND COOK INLET

Dave Musgrave, Ph.D.

School of Fisheries and Ocean Sciences, University of Alaska Fairbanks
P.O. Box 757220, Fairbanks AK 99709-7220
(907) 474-7837, Email: musgrave@ims.uaf.edu

Presented by Mr. Hank Statscewich.

Our primary goal with this project is to obtain spatial and temporal surface circulation fields for a portion of lower Cook Inlet and the central Beaufort Sea shelf in the vicinity of offshore oil production. These measurements will contribute to the baseline oceanography of two regions where few *in situ* current measurements have been made, and will therefore help to promote the general understanding of surface currents in these areas. These investigations will be an important undertaking for the Minerals Management Service (MMS) future efforts to model potential oil spills and for possible spill response and oil spill contingency planning. The data can also be used by MMS for model comparison and validation, for both hydrodynamic models as well as general circulation models. By disseminating the data over the Internet in real-time, these data will assist professional users with a need for information for ship tracking and touring, coastal zone management, sediment transport, search and rescue operations, oil spill and other pollutant response.

An important objective is to evaluate the sensitivity of the instruments to measure surface currents within mixed ice and open water conditions (limited fetch conditions), under periods of high fresh water outflow from the river systems, during the development of spring/summer shore leads, and during the fall freeze-up and the formation of landfast ice in the nearshore Beaufort Sea. Oil spill trajectory models typically derive their wind measurements from either coastal meteorological stations or from satellite derived barometric pressure fields. These data do not provide true surface current measurements in mixed ice and open water conditions when fetch is limited. HF Doppler radar would provide significantly more accurate surface current measurements under these fetch-limited conditions.

Once the data is acquired, objectives include:

- Assessing effects of sea ice concentration and extent on collection of surface current measurements from HF Doppler radar.
- Validating the HF Doppler radar surface current data measurement by comparing these data against the subsurface current measurements from the Acoustic Doppler Current Profilers (ADCPs).
- Comparing and contrasting wind measurements from MMS or other adjacent coastal meteorological stations against the HF radar surface current measurements.
- Developing a web site and ground capability to monitor system integrity and performance and providing near real-time dissemination of surface current field data, vector maps, and surface current animations.
- Providing detailed analysis of current and tidal variability and system response from the HF Doppler radar. Determining the dynamics and variability of surface current circulation. Including any sea ice, bathymetry, meteorological, ADCP, drifter, tidal, sea surface temperature or other important comparative data that has been collected within the study area.

This study consists of two seasons of HF radar deployments in the Beaufort Sea and one year in Cook Inlet. In the Beaufort Sea we will deploy HF radar surface current mappers at two sites from June to October in 2005 and 2006. In October 2006, we will transport the two HF radar units to Cook Inlet where they will be deployed until November 2007. We will collect analyze, disseminate over the Internet, and archive surface current vector measurements. In the Beaufort Sea, data will be collected over a distance approximately 10-50 km from shore with a resolution of approximately 250 m to 3 km and will be used to resolve circulation patterns landward (inside) and seaward (outside) of any barrier islands. In Cook Inlet we will obtain quality controlled surface current vector measurements over a radial distance that is approximately 50-80 km from shore with a resolution of 1-3 km.

Discussion:

Ralph Cheng: I enjoyed your talk. There is a new program coming on line in California. They will be installing 40 of these CODAR units along the coast and San Francisco Bay. My question for you is that you showed example in Cook Inlet and you showed the current measured by CODAR behind an island. How can you get that information?

Hank Statscewich: Yes. That's a great point. We were really surprised when we saw radial returns from behind Kalgin Island. And what we found out, by basically blind luck, is that when you have very low lying islands which are basically salt marsh... The way that these signals propagate is that they couple basically to the ocean surface. You need a salty conductive medium. What happens is that it can see over barrier islands or small salt marshy-type of islands. So the ground type is extremely important for successful current measuring. And that's why we were able to see over Kalgin Island. It's a low-lying island, not very many trees, so the signal attenuation is very low from that area. We did have a big problem in Cook Inlet because the tidal range is so high; there is a six-meter tide. So that the wetting and drying problem that everybody has been talking about caused us a great headache. Because during the very, very low tides, there would be a lot of drying and our signal was attenuating. We were getting hardly any returns from our southern site because there is almost two kilometers of dry earth that the signal had to get over before it could couple to the ocean. That's just a learning curve that we had to work with in dealing with Alaska.

Tal Ezer: In the Cook Inlet area, the assumption behind the measurements is that the flow is wind driven. What happens in Cook Inlet when you have strong flow that is driven by the tide? So suppose there is no wind at all, will you be able to detect the flow?

Hank Statscewich: The underlying principle isn't for wind-driven circulation. The underlying principle is that you need surface waves.

Tal Ezer: What if there are no waves?

Hank Statscewich: If there are no waves, this doesn't work. But everywhere in the ocean we have waves. And so Cook Inlet is connected to the ocean, albeit, from upper Cook Inlet it's pretty far away. But there are many, many ocean waves, of all frequencies, that are propagating up Cook Inlet. They make a situation such that we are still able to measure the waves because it's connected by the open boundary at the southern end to the open ocean. So if there is no wind for a couple days, and it becomes very damp and you look out and it looks like a pond, even though your eye seems to perceive that there are no waves, we can tell that our instrument is measuring the waves that have very short periods, half a second, sometimes one second. They're just capillary waves.

Tal Ezer: What happens, for example, if you have a strong tidal currents going along the inlet? On the other hand, you have a cross flow from wind-driven? Which one do you actually measure?

Hank Statscewich: It integrates both. If you have a strong, tidally driven flow with waves on top, we only measure one component of the motion. And that is the one that's on a radial line from where our transceiver is located. So when you have two, now you are able to resolve that current in two dimensions. And so you have a wind-force component, you may have a baroclinic component associated with fresh water, and then you have a tidally driven component. This integrates all of the forcing mechanisms and tells us what the underlying current is. And so it's an average of all the different effects that may be forcing a current.

Warren Horowitz: The data will be, as Hank said, readily available to the scientific community, which hopefully will have the data on-line. And hopefully it will be deployed this June, beginning with the formation of the coastal leads.

Fate and Effects

CONTINUATION OF ARCTIC NEARSHORE IMPACT MONITORING IN DEVELOPMENT AREA (cANIMIDA): OVERVIEW

Gregory Durell

Battelle Memorial Institute, 397 Washington Street, Duxbury, MA 02332
(781) 934-0571, Fax (781) 934-2124, Email: durell@battelle.org

Dr. Richard Prentki, MMS, presented this talk at the Barrow IUM.

The Arctic Nearshore Impact Monitoring in Development Area (ANIMIDA), a five-year study started in 1999, provided baseline data and monitoring results for chemical contamination, turbidity, and subsistence whaling in the vicinity of Northstar and Liberty development sites. Northstar is in State waters, but includes production of some OCS oil through directional drilling. Liberty, if approved, will be the first offshore OCS development project in the Beaufort Sea and the Alaska OCS. ANIMIDA monitoring for Northstar included pre-construction, and construction, and early production periods. The last field sampling for ANIMIDA was conducted in 2003. In 2004 the five-year *Continuation* of Arctic Nearshore Impact Monitoring in Development Area (cANIMIDA) study began, and included spring and summer field surveys.

The cANIMIDA Program will gather baseline and long term monitoring data to evaluate potential effects from site-specific production in the Beaufort Sea OCS. Currently, these site-specific areas include the Northstar and Liberty areas; other prospects would be included if proposed for development. The cANIMIDA technical task objectives will include the following:

1. Hydrocarbon and metal characterization of sediments in the study area.
2. Sources, concentrations, and dispersion pathways for suspended sediment, and associated chemical constituents.
3. Partitioning of potential contaminants between dissolved and particulate phases.
4. Characterization of contaminants in amphipods, bivalves, and fish, and determination of bioaccumulation and effects of anthropogenic contaminants on biota.
5. Monitoring the Boulder Patch ecological system.
6. Annual assessment of subsistence whaling near Cross Island.

Field logistics include helicopter support and small vessel (e.g., MMS Launch 1273) support in the "open" water season and snow machine support in winter/spring. Turbidity, total suspended sediment, and current velocity measurements are being made in the vicinity of off- and on-shore potential sources, including local rivers and in the Boulder Patch. Sediment and suspended sediment samples will be analyzed for PAH, saturated hydrocarbons, chemical tracers, trace metals, and supporting geophysical measurements. Biota sampling includes contaminant measurements in clams, amphipods, deployed mussels, and fish, and also measurement of biological effects markers in fish bile and organ tissue. Kelp productivity is monitored in the Boulder Patch and uses the inherent optical properties of the ice and water to evaluate the effect of sediment resuspension on kelp productivity. Optical-related measurements include spectral irradiance, light scattering coefficients, and total suspended solids. The reporting program for Cross Island whaling, which records information on whaling locations, success, and whaler perceptions, is supported. Field programs will be scheduled in 2004-2006, with a possibility to extend to 2007. The last year of the Program will be devoted to reporting of monitoring results.

No Discussion.

Discussion at the Barrow IUM:

Doreen Lampe: Who are your contractors? Can you give us an example of one?

Dick Prentki: The core contractor for this study is Battelle, which is a nonprofit scientific organization. Michael Galginaitis of Applied Sociocultural Research is another one of the contractors on this. LGL is a third one.

Doreen Lampe: Who is going to report to you? What type of reports do they do? Do they make recommendations for less work or more work? Or just report "no significant findings"?

Dick Prentki: The contractors, the people doing the study, report to me as their contact at MMS. We get annual progress reports from them that may or may not have any recommendations. The final report will have scientific recommendations in it. They will tell us what is happening. If they see any problems they will be mentioned. They probably would not put forth a solution if they do find a problem. If they do find a problem, they will point that out and indicate if they think it is a problem or not. That work will go out to peer review and would be readily available to the North Slope Borough. The data from these studies will be available on a CD in the back of the reports. We are also making it available on the MMS website. All the data and analyses will be available to everyone.

George Olemaun: When you see contaminants, can you determine if the source is local or if it is airborne?

Dick Prentki: For some of the contaminants, like polycyclic aromatic hydrocarbons or the trace metals, we can probably do that. Under the original ANIMIDA study, we also looked at some of the persistent organic pollutants. We are not doing that in the current study. Those are probably from the rest of the world, not produced locally. We measured some of those concentrations, but we did not do any source studies. Some we can and some we cannot. If we think it could be a local source, we can identify that. We will look for local sources. If it is not local, we won't be chasing it any farther.

Craig George: From being involved in the Endicott project a number of years ago, one of the long-term effects that was predicted was that the causeway would cause the delta to silt up, build up shoals farther offshore, etc. Is your program following that?

Dick Prentki: We have not been involved in those studies. But from what I have seen up there, it has done both of those things. The Coastal Marine Institute at UAF may be compiling some industry data on that issue within the next year. BP is going to work with the university to look at some of the bathymetry data around Endicott. That is one of the issues that we have asked them to address. cANIMIDA has not done that, though.

Craig George: The last time I was through there, it looked like there was some shoaling building up inside in the Endicott lagoon.

Dick Prentki: There are some shoals inside and just offshore of Endicott too.

Craig George: In your results, it looks like you are not finding any obvious point sources of contaminants or anything?

Dick Prentki: No. However, we have one station offshore which appears to have a diesel oil signal; just one station out of probably 75 that we have looked at. It has had a contaminant signal that appears to be disappearing slowly. But it has been found consistently near the Liberty area.

Craig George: We are looking at hydrocarbons in bowhead whales. So far, with Dr. John Reynolds of Mote Marine Lab, they have not detected any petroleum-based compounds in bowheads. That is good news, but that was unexpected. Even a natural seep or some contact should show up.

Dick Prentki: Most of the mammals, I guess, can get rid of some of the hydrocarbons.

THE MMS cANIMIDA PROGRAM: HYDROCARBON CHEMISTRY OF SEDIMENTS IN THE NEARSHORE BEAUFORT SEA

John Brown[1], Paul Boehm[1], Linda Cook[1], John Trefry[2], and Greg Durell[3]

[1]Exponent, Inc. 2 Clock Tower Place, Maynard, MA 01754
(978) 461-1221, Fax (978) 461-1223, E-mail: jsbrown@exponent.com
[2]Florida Institute of Technology, Melbourne, FL 32901
[3]Battelle, 397 Washington Street, Duxbury, MA 02332

Hydrocarbon chemistry is one component of the multidisciplinary MMS cANIMIDA Program. The hydrocarbon chemistry study has focused on sediments and biota (clams and amphipods) from the nearshore Beaufort Sea. During the 1999, 2000, 2002 and 2004 summer field seasons, surface sediments were collected from stations throughout the study area, including site-specific stations adjacent to the Northstar and Liberty prospects. In the summer of 2001, sediment core samples were collected from suspected depositional areas to evaluate the historical record of nearshore sediments. The samples were analyzed for a full suite of hydrocarbons useful in determining petroleum contamination, including: saturated hydrocarbons, polynuclear aromatic hydrocarbons (PAH), and chemical biomarkers (steranes and triterpanes). The hydrocarbon data are being used to develop a monitoring database that can identify potential trends and inputs of petroleum contamination in the region and the development areas.

The 1999 hydrocarbon data serve as an important pre-development baseline for the Northstar and Liberty area. The 1999 results reveal that the area sediments generally contain low levels of naturally occurring background hydrocarbons, consistent with historical data from 1989 and earlier Beaufort Sea Monitoring Programs. Two stations with small increases in petroleum hydrocarbons, likely due to anthropogenic inputs, were identified in the 1999 data set. The post-Northstar construction data generally revealed no differences in sediment hydrocarbon concentrations or composition between the 1999 and 2000 - 2002 data sets. However, a subset of Northstar stations showed an increase in several key hydrocarbon parameters from 1999 to 2000. Detailed evaluation of the Northstar station data indicated that the observed trend showed no shift to anthropogenic hydrocarbon inputs, and was likely a function of the depletion of fine-grained sediments (and associated hydrocarbons) in 1999 due to storm activity, and not due to the development at Northstar Island. The 2001 sediment core results revealed low sedimentation rates in the study area (~0.1 cm/year to no recent deposition), supporting previous findings that the overall nearshore study area is a net erosional environment. The data from a subset of sediment cores where deposition rates can be well established, generally show uniform levels and distributions of background hydrocarbons extending back some 50 years and greater, with no discernable increases from recent offshore development activities.

The overall hydrocarbon data set can also be compared to sediment quality guidelines to gain a preliminary assessment of potential adverse effects to biota. No exceedences of petroleum hydrocarbon sediment quality guidelines have been noted thus far (1999 through 2002). Preliminary results from the 2004 field season sediments reveal hydrocarbon levels within the range of previous years, and no concentrations exceeding sediment quality guidelines.

Discussion:

Bill Streever: Thanks for the really well organized presentation. That was great. I have a couple of questions, though. I'd be interested to know how does this work compare to similar work that MMS is supporting, or anyone is supporting, say, in the Gulf of Mexico or the North Sea? And, secondly, I'm wondering what are the management trigger points? You have a very sensitive way to measure change, but maybe I missed something, but I didn't hear anything about at what level do we become concerned.

John Brown: To answer your first question: this is similar to some of the other programs that are going on in the Gulf of Mexico. Beyond that, data comparison-wise, the unusual part to the Beaufort Sea sediments is that there is a very prominent petroleum hydrocarbon signature that occurs naturally in the sediments. And I don't know if that answers your question, but it is a little bit different in that we are finding naturally occurring petroleum. Now, there are areas in the Gulf of Mexico where there are natural seeps, etc. There are programs have certainly identified areas in the Gulf, at least ones that I've been involved with, not so much with MMS but with the American Petroleum Institute, where there's petroleum contamination of Gulf sediments. We're not finding that here, so hopefully that answers your first question.

Your second question is what are the trigger mechanisms. I guess the trigger mechanisms are really the forums such as this one, as well as the reports and publications that we generate. Now, we haven't had one *per se* because we haven't had an exceedence. If, for example, next year, we find out that Northstar is up 250%, and all our statistical analyses show that there's a problem, then that's going to be in MMS's report. In other words, that's the trigger mechanism to get that out there. It goes in the reports and publications to MMS. And we don't call up the Anchorage Daily News, if that's the question. But ultimately it's reported to MMS. And Cleve probably has something to say on that.

Cleve Cowles: Just as a follow-up, as part of the design of this project, and from the guidance that our scientific committee gave us a few years ago, we developed what we call a "decision linkage matrix" for this project. For each of the tasks in the project, there is a defined hypothesis or statement linked to an issue. Should there be a significant change, the Contracting Officer's Technical Representative will be notified and then, through that linkage, our regional management team, such as the regional director and his regional supervisors, would be advised of the information, They would then compare it to whatever regulatory responsibility that our agency has or other agencies that might need to be informed. So we do have a process by which there are considerations of new information as it comes in, and it's handled through our internal experts and authorities.

John Brown: Just so you know, this is an example of the decision matrix that Cleve is talking about (Slide showing matrix is shown). I mentioned, I think, at the very start of the presentation, ultimately the communication; the trigger mechanism is here, where we generate reports to MMS, and then MMS disseminates the information.

Unidentified: You showed the proportion of the pyrogenic PAHs going up over your sampling period, so either they're going up or something else is going down. Which is it?

John Brown: Right. That's a subtle shift. You have to remember the pyrogenics represent slightly less slightly less than 50% of the total. You have to remember that our analytical variability in the total wobbles quite a bit. In other words, if there is simply an incremental addition of pyrogenics and the petrogenics remain the same, we would probably be hard-pressed to measure that, at this point. However, we are capable of measuring it through the ratio, as a total. But through the ratio, we are capable of measuring it. But right now I have to answer that in saying, you are right, the overall, on average, the overall total PAH concentrations in the region have not changed. So it looks like, by definition, if the pyrogenics are going up, the petrogenics are going down slightly.

Unidentified: All data were surrogate corrected, that you showed, or not?

John Brown: Actually, all those data were surrogate corrected

Unidentified: All your normalizations were done with silt/clay fraction rather than total organic carbon (TOC)? And I was wondering how much worse was the regression with TOC, and whether the increase in pyrogenics normalized the silt and clay, also as seen normalized to TOC? In other words, whether changing TOC could be a factor in driving the increased pyrogenics.

John Brown: The reason we normalize the silt/clay fraction is because the TOC measurements here are so variable that the line becomes flat. The R^2 is so bad you can't use it. However, one of the novel techniques we use, and we're actually looking into and will apply it, I haven't had the chance to do it to 2004 data, is to actually use one of the analytical tracers that is the most abundant in our study perylene, and normalize to perylene. And we found that, actually, perylene is a better normalizer than silt/clay, with one exception. There's a station 4A that doesn't fit the model. But think if we start using perylene, that actually we'll get a better normalization, the R^2 goes way up. It is much better than silt/clay, because we're actually using one of the instruments we used to measure the all other data to actually normalize. However, that shouldn't affect the ratio *per se*, although we... I take that back, we can normalize to perylene, and then use the ratio, but the ratio excludes perylene. It's one of those weird, borderline situations. I mean, you can find it in very minor petrogenic sources, and certainly you can find it in pyrogenic sources.

SOURCES, CONCENTRATIONS AND DISPERSION PATHWAYS FOR SUSPENDED SEDIMENTS and PARTITIONING OF POTENTIAL POLLUTANTS BETWEEN DISSOLVED AND PARTICULATE PHASES

John H. Trefry[1], Robert P. Trocine[1], Matthew B. Alkire[1], Debra W. Woodall[1], Robert D. Rember[2], Mark Savoie[3] and Gregory Durell[4]

[1]Department of Marine & Environmental Systems, Florida Institute of Technology
Melbourne, FL 32901, (321) 674-7305, Fax (321) 674-7212, E-mail: jtrefry@fit.edu
[2]IARC, University of Alaska, Fairbanks, AK, 99775
[3]Kinnetics Laboratories, Inc., 403 West Eighth Avenue, Anchorage, AK 99501
[4]Battelle, 397 Washington Street, Duxbury, MA 02332

This component of the cANIMIDA project was designed to study suspended sediments as well as dissolved and particulate metals and hydrocarbons. Suspended sediments, a dynamic and complex component in the environmental framework of the coastal Beaufort Sea, consist of both inorganic and biogenic fractions and are linked to levels of dissolved chemicals. The primary question addressed in this study is: Will offshore oil development and production in the coastal Beaufort Sea result in increased or chronic loadings of suspended sediments or particulate and dissolved contaminant metals or hydrocarbons? In addition, a fundamental goal for this study is to gain an understanding of the natural sources, concentrations and transport pathways of chemicals in the cANIMIDA area and their uptake by organisms.

Winter is marked by concentrations of total suspended sediments (TSS) under the ice that average ~0.2 mg/L. The winter calm is disrupted when >80% of the TSS delivered annually to the Beaufort Sea by rivers occurs in 2-3 weeks during May-June when TSS in rivers reaches 600 mg/L. Most of the river water is carried to a frozen Beaufort Sea where the discharge forms a 1-2 m thick channel under the ice. During spring 2004, the under-ice flow from the Sagavanirktok and Kuparuk rivers was tracked and sampled at 28 locations. Optimum multiparameter analysis with salinity, temperature, $\delta^{18}O$ and dissolved silica shows the relative contributions of each river, sea-ice melt and the offshore polar mixed layer to the under-ice flow. Flow patterns are used to track the offshore transport of freshwater, suspended sediment, organic carbon, nutrients and dissolved and particulate trace metals. The study also provides insight for transport pathways of any under-ice spills that may occur at this dynamic time of year. Levels of TSS during the open-water period are related to wind speed, wave height and the presence of sea ice. At near calm, TSS is ~1-4 mg/L, with increases to 60-80 mg/L after 2-3 days of winds greater than 20 knots.

A complementary component of the program is to determine levels of dissolved and particulate metals (As, Ba, Cd, Cr, Cu, Hg, Pb and Zn) in snow, rivers, under ice, and in open water. Concentrations of dissolved metals in river water during spring floods increase in response to flushing of dissolved organic matter from decaying vegetation associated with soils and surface ponds. Snow has concentrations of metals that are 10- to 25-fold lower than dissolved levels in the rivers at peak discharge. Levels of dissolved metals in the saline waters of the Beaufort Sea are generally lower than found in the rivers with seawater Pb at 4-7 ng/L, Cu at 0.5 µg/L and Ba at 13 µg/L. Concentrations of dissolved metals and organic substances offshore are controlled by adsorption on suspended sediment and by biological uptake.

Discussion:

Hajo Eicken: What is the fraction of river water that is transported on top of the ice, relative to underneath, during spring break-up?

John Trefry: I don't know the exact answer. If I had to guess, I'd say 25%. You never get the water coming as far offshore on top of the ice as you do under it. And the thickness of the water on the ice is usually relatively thin, and there's some back draining of the water back into the open water. I don't have the data even to make that calculation, but it should be a relatively small fraction.

Hajo Eicken: How important is resuspension of marine sediments as a result of drainage of strudel holes or drainage through cracks and other slots? Is that going to impact some of the data that you showed?

John Trefry: We have not sampled near a strudel hole, and we have not seen high concentrations of suspended sediment in the bottom water. So there's a pretty good disconnect in most locations between that meter and a half of river water on the bottom, several meters. We have not seen really very enhanced concentrations. It would fun to find the right strudel hole and do that. Other people have done some of that. It would certainly have an effect on resuspending some sediment, of course. That's a bigger issue of how much sediment is resuspended and advected out of the area completely. We think that's very large.

Mike Castellini: If you look at, what I would call, the transport per time of your metals that would be the product of concentration times flow. Does that normalize every single one of them so that they're always all lined up the same? Are you getting some chemicals that are released even though they're not at the time of maximum flow? Do you see what I'm trying to say there?

John Trefry: Right. Take for example, barium. Barium really doesn't change in concentration very much during flow. It changes only in effect through a dilution. As the run-off goes out, the actual barium concentration goes down a little bit. So it's very uniform all the way along the line. See, there're a lot of just less reactive chemicals that have not been leached out of the soil. Barium doesn't get leached out of the soil. But it's just going along at a relatively constant rate. Calcium and other major elements tend to go along at a constant rate.

INTEGRATED BIOMONITORING AND BIOACCUMULATION OF ANTHROPOGENIC COMPOUNDS IN BIOTA OF THE cANIMIDA STUDY AREA

Jerry M. Neff

Battelle Memorial Institute, 397 Washington St., Duxbury, MA 02332
(781) 952-5229, Fax (781) 934-2124, E-mail: neffjm@battelle.org

---

Task 5 of the cANIMIDA Project was designed to determine the bioavailability and potential for trophic transfer of selected metals and petroleum hydrocarbons (polycyclic aromatic hydrocarbons [PAH], saturated hydrocarbons, and sterane/triterpane biomarkers) in marine invertebrates and fish from the vicinity of the Northstar and Liberty development prospects in the Alaskan Beaufort Sea. Thirteen metals (Ag, As, Ba, Cd, Cr, Cu, Fe, Hg, Ni, Pb, Se, V, and Zn), more than 40 PAH (naphthalene – benzo(ghi)perylene plus several alkyl homologues), saturated hydrocarbons, and petroleum biomarkers were measured in soft tissues of seven species of fish, clams (*Astarte*), and amphipods (*Anonyx*). PAH metabolites in bile and cytochrome P450 activity (CYP1A) in several tissues (biomarkers of PAH exposure) were measured in fish. The abundance and species composition of the fish community is highly variable at different sampling sites, making geographic comparisons of residue and enzyme data difficult.

Metals concentrations in tissues of fish, clams, and amphipods are comparable to concentrations in similar species from uncontaminated marine environments. Concentrations of most metals are lowest in fish tissues, intermediate in amphipods, and highest in clams. There is little interannual variation since 1986 in metals concentrations in tissues of amphipods and clams.

Concentrations of PAH also are low in animals from the study area, particularly in tissues of the seven species of fish. Among the fish species, highest concentratons are in four horned sculpin. Clams and amphipods also contain low concentrations of PAH. The PAH assemblage in the marine animal tissues is characteristic of mixed petrogenic/pyrogenic sources. Significant CYP1A activity is present only in hepatocytes of Arctic cisco and least cisco. Highest activity is in hepatocytes of Arctic cisco from Point Brower (near the Liberty prospect and Endicott). A single four horned sculpin (of 3 replicates) from Tigvariak Island has elevated hepatic CYP1A. The PAH residue and CYP1A data indicate a low level of exposure to PAH.

Discussion:

John Brown: I just have a comment. You had good data for two cisco up there. Those are two species that are highly transient. You got them at Brower, but it really doesn't matter. If they show induction, you don't know whether it was induction from oil operations or something they were exposed to in the Colville River or whatever their home river might be.

Jerry Neff: I agree. And that's the problem with using wild fish. Of course, the sculpin is probably the best because they are fairly resident, as you mentioned before the meeting, and they're long-lived. Most of the other fish are juveniles coming out of the rivers or migrating along the coast. That's the trouble with using a wild fish, in particular, because they're highly migratory. You never know where they were yesterday and whether they picked up their induction somewhere else. The bivalves are less a problem in that way. The amphipods, again, are the same thing. You don't know where they've been. And so it's difficult to use them for monitoring.

LONG-TERM MONITORING OF THE KELP COMMUNITY IN THE STEFANSSON SOUND BOULDER PATCH: DETECTION OF CHANGE RELATED TO OIL AND GAS DEVELOPMENT

Ken Dunton[1], Dale Funk[2], and Katrin Iken[3]

[1]The University of Texas Marine Science Institute, 750 Channel View Drive, Port Aransas, TX 78373, (361) 749-6728, Fax (361) 749-6777, E-mail: dunton@utmsi.utexas.edu;
[2]LGL Alaska Research Associates, Inc., 1101 East 76th Ave., Suite B, Anchorage, Alaska 99518 (907) 562-3339; Fax (907) 562-7223; E-mail: dfunk@lgl.com;
[3]University of Alaska, Institute of Marine Science, Fairbanks, AK 99701 (907) 474-5192; E-mail: iken@ims.uaf.edu

---

The continuation of long-term monitoring of kelp and the associated invertebrate community in Stefansson Sound Boulder Patch is designed to address ecosystem change as related to anthropogenic activities from oil and gas development. The initial effort under the Arctic Nearshore Impact Monitoring in the Development Area (ANIMIDA) was focused on establishing a quantitative relationship between total suspended solids (TSS) and benthic kelp productivity. Under the continuation of this program (cANIMIDA), the following objectives are addressed: 1) define the spatial variability in annual productivity and biomass of kelp; 2) monitor incident and *in situ* ambient light (as photosynthetically active radiation [PAR]) and TSS; 3) establish the quantitative relationship between TSS, light attenuation, and kelp productivity; 4) measure benthic faunal community diversity; 5) incorporate historical datasets related to kelp productivity, ambient PAR measurements (both surface and underwater), and benthic diversity into ANIMIDA datasets to establish a long-term record available in digital format, and 6) develop a rationale and strategy for future Boulder Patch contaminant monitoring. For cANIMIDA, three sampling strategies are used over three summers from 2004-2006: 1) generate semi-synoptic maps of TSS and light attenuation parameters through sampling of ca. 30 randomly-selected points in a 300 km^2 area that includes the Boulder Patch and the region south of Narwhal Island to the Sagavanirktok Delta; 2) monitor long-term variations in underwater PAR at four fixed sites and incident PAR at one coastal site during the summer open-water period; and 3) re-visit seven monitoring stations established during the 1984-1991 Boulder Patch Monitoring Program (LGL Ecological Research Associates and Dunton, 1992) for measurement of benthic faunal diversity in 2005 and 2006. In addition to simultaneous measurements of PAR and TSS, other parameters measured include water column chlorophyll and dissolved inorganic nitrogen and phosphorus. At the fixed sites, continuous PAR measurements will be made over three summers. At three of these sites, continuous PAR measurements were collected from 1986 to 1991, providing an important baseline from which to detect long-term change. Collection of benthic diversity data at seven stations originally surveyed from 1984 to 1991 will be supplemented with kelp biomass measurements to provide for more accurate estimates of kelp productivity. Synoptic measurements of TSS and light attenuation coefficients collected over both spatial and temporal scales will be inserted into a productivity model to estimate annual kelp production throughout the Boulder Patch. Daily production estimates in response to light attenuation changes can be estimated at fixed sites to provide valuable baseline data on temporal variations characteristic of different Boulder Patch areas. Data collected in this program combined with historical measurements will provide a valuable database from which to assess ecosystem change in response to oil and gas activities in the region.

Literature Cited:

LGL Ecological Research Associates, Inc. and K. Dunton. 1992. Endicott Beaufort Sea Boulder Patch Monitoring Program (1990-1991). Unpubl. Rep. by LGL, Inc., Bryan, TX for BP Exploration (Alaska), Inc., Anchorage, AK. 153 p. plus appendices.

Discussion:

Jerry McCutcheon: Your five million metric tons of sediment by the Colville River; are you sure of that?

Ken Dunton: Yes, I am. John Trefry came up with the same number recently.

Jerry McCutcheon: Cook Inlet has 200,000 tons. That's just an awful lot more than all of Cook Inlet.

Ken Dunton: I'm very aware of that. The amount of eroded sediments deposited in the coastal zone of the Beaufort Sea is amazing. That's for the Colville, which is the largest river on the Arctic slope. That's a good number. I can give you a reference for that. It's in the literature.

Hajo Eicken: What do you think of the impact of a longer open-water season and potentially less snow on the sea ice, a shorter ice season, on production of kelp? Is that going to potentially offset some of this increased turbidity that you are seeing in the summer?

Ken Dunton: That's a good question. I have thought about that, Hajo. In terms of the longer open-water season, the kelp should benefit, particularly if the ice breaks up earlier. Not in the fall, but certainly in the spring. But with the ice cover in the spring, and since there's so much sediment in the ice canopy there's no light underneath the ice, so an earlier break-up should make a difference for these plants. But the same time, if there is an earlier break-up, if it means that we're just going to have a higher intensity of storms, increased erosion, and more sediment in the water column, it may get cancelled out. But that's a good question, one that we've been debating around the table quite a bit.

Unidentified: When you superimposed the temporal pattern of the irradiance and total suspended solids (TSS), does TSS peak slightly before the peak in irradiance? I'm trying to think about how TSS is influencing that as a function of the growth period.

Ken Dunton: The TSS variation is all due to summer storms. Early in the season, right after break-up, TSS levels are relatively high but they drop off real quickly. After that point, peaks in TSS during the summer time are due entirely to storms.

Unidentified: So the dominant TSS effect on reducing irradiance is really the storms as opposed to the spring push?

Ken Dunton: Exactly.

Bodil Bluhm: Could you comment on the role of the Boulder Patch for the environment around it? Say there's no Boulder Patch anymore. What would be the effect? Is there exchanged dispersal of larvae, for example, of critical fish habitat or something that where the Boulder Patch affects the surrounding environment? Would the demise of the Boulder Patch have and effect on Beaufort Sea coast ecosystem?

Ken Dunton: I would like to say, if the Boulder Patch is gone, the whole ecosystem is going to crash. But that is perhaps true for the Aleutians with the *Selendang Ayu,* for the kelp bed that took a big hit, the whole sea otter story, with killer whales in the Aleutians. We did lose quite an ecosystem there. This not a big enough community to have any significant impact on fisheries or higher trophic levels in the Beaufort Sea. It's just too small. I think its significance that it is unique and it is isolated. And it is the only feature like it in, probably, over a thousand kilometers of coastline, from Demarcation Bay onto the Siberian side. We've identified quite a few new species there. I'm sure a lot are going to be identified in the future. I don't think it's critical for the Beaufort Sea coast, in terms of an ecosystem, in terms of losing Arctic char, Arctic cisco, etc. I don't think those species spend time in there. And I recollect that someone said something about polar bears diving down and eating kelp. But I don't think polar bears are really depending very heavily on getting their salad in the Boulder Patch.

Bill Streever: I wonder if you could talk a little bit about repercussions, as you see them, for oil development in the Beaufort Sea, and how you might manage things like sediment resuspension during dredging, and even if that would matter, and related issues?

Ken Dunton: Good question. It's very interesting. I deal with these same questions and issues in the Gulf of Mexico coast with respect to sea grasses, and dredging in the Intercoastal Waterway. There is a sea grass conservation plan for the State of Texas where the sea grasses are very threatened by sediment resuspension events which are mostly caused by dredging. And what we have done is restrict dredging to the winter months, when the plants are not physiologically active. In the Beaufort Sea, I would suggest that, along those same lines, the construction activities take place during the winter period, during the ice-covered period, not during the summer. Obviously the summer time is when they're photosynthesizing. We used silt curtains for dredging activities in the Gulf. I would recommend that the industry here do their very best to minimize erosion through the use of hard protection on causeways, on islands, etc. Those are two ideas that come right to mind; just minimizing erosion and therefore resuspension, and secondly, restricting activities, the majority of activities, to the winter period. We know that these plants rely very heavily on what goes on in the summer time. If the ice was clear, it would be a different story, but the ice is not clear in the wintertime in the Boulder Patch. It's very turbid, as you know, and so there's no light penetration with the ice canopy. That's in contrast with the Antarctic, of course, where we see perfectly well under the ice in the Antarctic. It's a completely different story. Those are the first things that come to mind.

Jerry McCutcheon: Can you visualize your five million metric tons of silt? Can you visualize it, quantify it somehow, and visualize it? What's it look like?

Ken Dunton: Can I visualize it? When you go out on the ice in the early spring, the ice is black. There's sediment all over the ice for miles and miles around. As you fly a helicopter along the coast, you basically see dirty ice everywhere you see. I can't recall the concentrations of sediment in the ice that we have measured, but it's pretty substantial. And on the seabed I see tremendous quantities of silt during the various times of the year, especially in the fall. So I can visualize it pretty well.

Jerry McCutcheon: How many railroad cars would it be?

Ken Dunton: Oh, my gosh! I have no idea. Quite a few.

Jerry McCutcheon: Not too hard to figure out. If you had a hundred-car train, it would be about a mile long, you'd have 12 hundred-car trains. You'd be half way to the Slope and half way back. Are you sure it's five million metric tons?

John Trefry: Do you know the volume of water that comes down the Colville River?

Jerry McCutcheon: No, I don't. I know the volume of water that comes down the Susitna River.

John Trefry: The folks from Baker Engineering did quite a lot of surveying around that area to look at flow.

Jerry McCutcheon: Do you know the volume of water that comes down the Susitna River? Is it greater or less than the Colville?

John Trefry: I do, but I don't have it with me. I don't know off the top of my head. I know what's coming down the Colville River today. I have the Susitna data elsewhere.

Jerry McCutcheon: [not audible]?

John Trefry: Very large. And so is the total amount of sediment...

Unidentified: So what is the river run-off, by the way?

John Trefry: I thought I was starting a conversation here. Anyway, the answer is about 15 cubic kilometers of water come down the Colville. I have measured levels of suspended sediment in the Colville as high as 1,000 milligrams per liter. Two-thirds or more of all the water is coming down in two to three weeks. The thing peaks and goes. If you have an average of just 400 milligrams per liter over that two to three weeks, you can make your five million tons. It's not very hard. I've been down that road quite a few times.

Unidentified: [not audible]?

John Trefry: The answer is about 15 cubic kilometers, that's Baker Engineering's number. Fifteen cubic kilometers. And I'm saying that if you average 400 milligrams per liter, you get your six tons. And it runs way above that, way above that at its peak. So, although it's a lot of train cars, there's a lot of mud. In contrast, the number for the Sagavanirktok is only a quarter of a megaton. The Colville's a whole different ball game than the Sagavanirktok. We wish we could do more work on the Colville. It's just so difficult to get to. And I do have the Susitna and Knik data, but not with me.

PERSISTENCE OF CRUDE OIL SPILLS ON OPEN WATER

Ian Buist[1], Randy Belore [1], Alun Lewis[2], Frank Bercha[3], Milan Cerovšek[3],
Justin Wilson[4], Bob Rinelli[4], and Dick Prentki[5]

[1]SL Ross Environmental Research Ltd., 200-717 Belfast Rd.Ottawa, ON Canada K1G 0Z4
(623) 232-1546, Fax (623) 232-6660, email: Ian@slross.com
[2]Alun Lewis Oil Spill Consultancy, United Kingdom
[3]Bercha Group, Calgary, AB
[4]PCCI, Alexandria, VA
[5]Minerals Management Service, Anchorage, AK

The Minerals Management Service (MMS) has environmental impact assessment responsibilities under both the National Environmental Policy Act (NEPA) and the Outer Continental Shelf Lands Act (OCSLA), which are partially addressed through the use of oil spill modeling. The analytical approach used by MMS includes a combination of trajectory modeling, oil weathering modeling, and correlations between spill size and length of coastline affected. Unfortunately, the correlations do not take into account spill persistence, and small spills, even far offshore, are presumed to be as likely to reach shorelines, as are large spills. This does not make intuitive sense and goes against the commonly held views of spill experts. MMS in Alaska is particularly concerned about the issue because scenarios currently considered in Lease Sale EIAs involve relatively small spills in the size range of 500 to 1000 barrels. The primary objective of this study was to develop mathematical descriptions of the persistence of crude oil spills at sea in open water, as a function of spill size, based on a statistical analysis of historical data.

An in-depth survey of reports of oil spill incidents throughout the world was completed. Major oil spill incidents since 1967 have generated an immense amount of literature, but reliable information on oil slick persistence is rare. Of the final incident list that met the study criteria, 13 were releases from tankers and 7 were oil well blowouts. In addition to these, a list of 12 small experimental spills was compiled, for which good data existed.

Correlation analyses were carried out on the three data sets and, although they by no means gave definitive results because of their small size, they did indicate the relative importance of different variables and their dependencies. Regression analysis with the three data sets showed that:

For spills greater than or equal to 1000 barrels in size:
$$PD_{\geq 1000bbl} = 0.0001S - 1.32T + 33.1$$

For spills less than 1000 barrels in size:
$$PD_{<1000bbl} = 0.0034S + 2.02$$

Where   PD = Spill persistence in days
      S = Spill size in barrels
      T = Water temperature in degrees Celsius

Neither wind speed nor countermeasures had a significant effect on persistence. Estimates of statistical significance and 95% confidence intervals for the predictors were calculated and cumulative distribution function plots were prepared for several spill sizes.

The above predictions apply to spills of most crude oils, with the notable exception of very light crudes, specifically those with an API Gravity exceeding 45.5°. Most very light crudes, or condensates, have pour points that are less than ambient temperature and are likely to dissipate in less than one day. A few of these oils have high pour points, and these would persist if they were spilled on water colder than their pour point.

Discussion:

Lois Epstein: I have a question about the fact that the correlation had two different components with the tanker spills but only one component with the blowout spills. And I'm wondering if that was a concern to you at all? Or did you hypothesize any particular difference between the tanker spills and the blowout spills? Why one would be impacted by temperature and the other one not?

Ian Buist: Probably the answer is that most of the blowouts have occurred in temperate waters; whereas as tanker spills have been spread out among cold, temperate, and tropical waters. So, within the database for the blowouts, there just was no distribution of temperatures, whereas in the vessel spills, there was.

Dick Prentki: Ian, we were afraid that you weren't going to find a lot of spills to work with, and you really didn't. But then, if they don't have information on the persistence of these spills, how are they cutting off spill clean up? If they're not following the spills until it quits persisting and documenting that, how are they deciding to quit cleaning up spills?

Ian Buist: Well, I think the thing to remember is that for a spill to make this database, it had to go out to sea. And someone had to keep going out to sea and flying over it and saying "It's still there, it's still there, oops, it's gone." And that became a recordable incident that was of use here. We did not look at spills that tended to just come ashore and then be cleaned up on shore. And that's where the big decisions about when to stop cleaning up come in which is an extremely difficult decision to make. So, I think most of these spills that made this database were... There wasn't a lot of response effort going on for the offshore spill. Somebody just kept flying out to find out where it was and see whether it had crossed an international border or.... But as long as it stayed offshore, it wasn't a problem.

John Petterson: I'm an anthropologist. Looking at the *Selendang Ayu* oil spill started December 7 and there is still concern about tar balls. So I was pleased to see your penultimate statement that, well, the tar balls can be out there, disrupting fisheries or having human consequences, but they're neither dissipated nor persistent, according to your frame of reference there. The issue of defining persistence and dissipation seems to be an issue from the social side.

Ian Buist: I think there's been quite a few recent heavy oil spills, particularly residual fuel oils, both industrial and marine fuel oils, that have opened people's eyes again to the fact that most computer models look at how a spill naturally disperses. Breaking waves fracture the slick into a range of drop sizes; the smallest ones become permanently dispersed. This continues until the spill dissipates. But maybe, for heavy crude oils, as well, it's a constant sort of spreading across the sea surface, and breaking down into ever-smaller surface particles. And then you just can't see it anymore from a plane. It's still there as small particles. And maybe for really heavy fuel oils, such as the spill in the Aleutians, they're being transported at some depth below the surface. And they come up when it's warm; they go down when it's cold. Persistence is very difficult to define for something like that.

Jim Bennett: Have you compared your results with other computer models that are available, like ASA's model?

Ian Buist: We specifically did not use any computer modeling in this project. It was to be strictly based on statistical analysis of real incidents for which there was legally defensible data, to say it survived this long at sea. So, no, we have not compared.

Walter Johnson: How many of the seven blowouts were in the U.S. Outer Continental Shelf waters? This was an international database?

Ian Buist: I would say maybe one or two.

Walter Johnson: One or two? And how long has it been since one occurred?

Ian Buist: A long time ago, in the 1970s.

Walter Johnson: There may be some technological aspects here too.

Ian Buist: I think there was one in the 1990s but wasn't in U.S. waters it was in state waters. It's been a long time since there was a blowout in U.S. OCS waters.

IMPROVEMENTS IN THE FAULT TREE APPROACH TO OIL SPILL OCCURRENCE ESTIMATORS FOR THE BEAUFORT SEA

Frank G. Bercha, Ph.D.

Bercha Group, 2926 Parkdale Blvd., NW, Calgary, AB, Canada T2N 3S9
(403) 270-2221, Fax (403) 270-2014, Email: berchaf@berchagroup.com

---

Occurrence estimators for oil spills are values of probabilities of occurrences of oil spills of different volumes, locations, causes, and times within different development and production scenarios. Because adequate historical data for characterizing Arctic marine oil spills are not available, a network simulation technique called fault tree analysis was used. The fault trees were first constructed to emulate the spill occurrence probabilities for a location of known history, primarily the Gulf of Mexico, and then modified to include Arctic effects. In Phase 1 of the work occurrence estimators were evaluated with specific focus on the uncertainties introduced from the consideration of Arctic effects such as ice gouging and strudel scour, but excluded consideration of the inherent uncertainties of the statistics for the known locations. In Phase 2, currently underway, the improvement is that both the uncertainties in spill frequencies and volumes derived from the base data and those for the Arctic effects are integrated to provide probabilistic distributions of the spill indicators. In this presentation, following a discussion of the Phase 1 and 2 methodologies, preliminary results of the spill indicators for a typical development scenario are presented, discussed, and preliminary conclusions are proposed.

Discussion:

Hajo Eicken: I was intrigued by your results that the occurrence of pipeline spills decreases with water depth. Are you assuming that a pipeline is buried at the mean scour depth for this analysis?

Frank Bercha: I don't recall that actually. But the reason for the decrease is that, first of all, the primary causal mechanism for spills is gouging. It's actually Arctic effects. But the dominant one there is gouging in the shallow and medium water depth. After that, the primary mechanism is the third party. We did make an assumption about the pipeline burial depth, which I can't recall. I'd have to look in my report.

Hajo Eicken: I guess that's the critical issue because as you go out to 20 meters water depth, the probability of gouging is more or less the same. It's on the order of once every two years on a point-base type of analysis. If you then assume that gouge depth increases with water depth, you would have to make some assumption about what is the depth of burial of the pipeline. If it were buried at mean depth, you would assume that the rate of gouging actually goes up, right?

Frank Bercha: I don't think that we took it at mean gouge depths. I think we took it beyond that. I think it was the 90%. It was the BP criterion, is what we used, from Liberty. I got that from Denis Blanchet. Quite frankly, I can't remember. We'll have to look at the original report.

John Petterson: If I understand this correctly, you used Gulf of Mexico and North Sea data on spills and the causes of those spills as the basis for your projection on the Arctic. And of those, the largest component was a third-party event. So that, in effect, your analysis of the North Slope spills, by subtracting that component out, yields a much larger likelihood. If you took both of those out, both the Gulf of Mexico and the North Slope, then the result would be the opposite. I'll talk to you about this.

Frank Bercha: If I took out the third party on both?

John Petterson: In both. The problem is that on the North Slope, it's nowhere near the benign environment of the Gulf of Mexico, as far as the environmental factors that influence a spill. That would be my answer.

Frank Bercha: Well, just a real quick comment, perhaps an elucidation. We did not remove the third party in the North Slope, we simply reduced it. Because when there's ice, it's unlikely to have anchors and so on. But we think we included a lot of the environmental impacts that are unique to the North Slope but do not exist in the Gulf of Mexico. It's certainly a subject you and I can discuss further.

EMPIRICAL WEATHERING PROPERTIES OF OIL IN SNOW AND ICE

Ian Buist[1], Randy Belore [1] Dan Hackenberg[2], Dave Devitis[2], David Dickins[3], Bruce Hollebone[3], Zhendi Wang[4] and Dick Prentki[5]

[1]SL Ross Environmental Research Ltd., 200-717 Belfast Rd.Ottawa, ON Canada K1G 0Z4
(623) 232-1546, Fax (623) 232-6660, email: Ian@slross.com
[2]Mar, Inc., Rockville, MD
[3]DF Dickins Associates, La Jolla, CA
[4]Environment Canada, Ottawa, ON
[5]Minerals Management Service, Anchorage, AK

MMS Alaska uses oil spill weathering models for National Environmental Policy Act (NEPA) analysis, as well as for preparing oil spill response strategies for Oil Discharge Prevention and Contingency Plans (ODPCPs). A considerable amount of field research was done in the 1970s and 1980s on first order physics of oil weathering in ice. Additional studies continued in the laboratory in the late 1980's and 1990's, but were generally limited to low-viscosity, low-pour point oils. It is now recognized that oil weathering is strongly dependent on the specific chemical composition and characteristics of individual crudes. The physical and chemical data required by modern state-of-the-art models (such as the SINTEF oil weathering model used by MMS in Alaska) are scarce, of poor quality, or nonexistent for oil-ice interaction.

The objective of the research is to generate experimental data that can be used to validate and refine weathering algorithms and computerized oil weathering models in the presence of ice and snow. More specifically the experiments will:

1. For low and high pour point oils, measure emulsification, evaporation, spreading, under-ice movement, slick thickness, and oil composition changes in an ice field and in snow on sea ice.
2. Develop a database on oil weathering in ice fields for use in model validation.
3. Use these data in concert with other oil-ice weathering data to validate and enhance or develop new algorithms of oil weathering in ice.

The emphasis for the research will be extensive laboratory testing with meso-scale verification to investigate the fate, behavior and interactions of fresh crude oil spilled with first-year, land-fast sea ice. Six series of experiments are planned over the next two years:

1. Spreading in Ice and Snow
2. Evaporation in Ice and Snow
3. Slick Thickness on Cold Water
4. Migration Rates through Brine Channels
5. Formation of Water-in-Oil Emulsions
6. Full Spill-Related Characterization of Crude Oil Samples

These experiments are being conducted at three facilities:

- An outdoor test facility near Ottawa constructed using insulated, IBC shipping containers as the test tanks each containing 1 m^3 of salt water.
- An indoor, 11-m^3 wind/wave tank at SL Ross specially modified: to incorporate a refrigerated cold air system to allow precise air temperature control to −30°C; to allow the growing of substantial thicknesses of sea ice; and, to generate under-ice water currents.
- The 10,000-m^3 Ohmsett Facility in Leonardo, NJ, outfitted with large-capacity industrial water chillers to ensure freezing water temperatures.

Four crude oils from the North Slope of Alaska and representing a wide range of physical properties, are being used in the research: Alaska North Slope sales crude from Pump Station #1 on the TAPS pipeline, Northstar sales crude, Endicott sales crude, and Kuparuk sales crude.

Discussion:

Frank Bercha: If you were to pick the most scale-dependent parameters in the experiments, what would those be? Because I'm very interested in the scale effect, knowing there is one in many phenomena such as ice mechanics. I mean, why do you want to go to a large scale?

Ian Buist: It's different for each process that you're looking at. I think for spreading, the scale is volume. Different things happen at different volumes. For processes that involve mixing energy, we really don't know how to scale that very well. There's been an incredible amount of work done on doing small-scale tests to look at emulsification, dispersion, that sort of thing. But you only get real answers if you either go out to sea and do an experiment, or do it in something the size of Ohmsett, where that wave action is... For example, in emulsification and dispersion, not only is the magnitude of the mixing energy important, it's the difference between the impact of the breaking wave, and then there's a relaxation time between breaking waves. And all of that becomes important. Did I answer your question?

Frank Bercha: I'll just make one comment. By scale effect I would mean the change in unit rates which occurs when you move from one scale to another. For maybe the emulsification rate might be a certain number and small scale, and on a large scale it becomes something different. That's kind of what I was getting at.

Ian Buist: Well, maybe I didn't answer your question then.

Biology

LARGE-SCALE MOVEMENTS AND HABITAT CHARACTERISTICS OF KING EIDERS THROUGHOUT THE NONBREEDING PERIOD

Laura M. Phillips[1], Abby N. Powell[1], and Eric Taylor[2]

[1]AK Coop. Fish and Wildlife Research Unit, University of Alaska, Fairbanks
209 Irving Building 1, Fairbanks, AK 99775
(907) 474-7144, Fax (907) 474-7872, email:fslmp@uaf.edu
[2]USFWS, Migratory Bird Management, Anchorage, AK

Alaskan-breeding King Eiders (*Somateria spectabilis*) molt wing feathers and over winter in remote areas of the Bering Sea, precluding direct observation. To characterize timing of migration and habitat used by King Eiders during the nonbreeding period, we collected location data of 60 individuals (27 females and 33 males) over three years from satellite telemetry and derived oceanographic information from remotely sensed data. Male King Eiders dispersed from breeding areas, arrived at wing molt sites, and dispersed from wing molt sites earlier than females in all years. Males that arrived at wing molt sites earlier also molted at higher latitudes. Female King Eiders that wintered farther south returned to breeding areas earlier the following summer. Distributions of molt and winter locations did not differ by sex or among years. We suggest that of the variables considered for analysis, distance to shore, water depth, and salinity best describe King Eider habitat throughout the nonbreeding period. King Eiders were located closer to shore, in shallower water with lower salinity than random locations. During the winter, lower ice concentrations were also associated with King Eider locations. This study provides some of the first large-scale descriptions of King Eider migration and habitat outside the breeding season.

No discussion.

SUSCEPTIBILITY OF SEA ICE BIOTA TO DISTURBANCES IN THE SHALLOW BEAUFORT SEA: PHASE 1: BIOLOGICAL COUPLING OF SEA ICE WITH THE PELAGIC AND BENTHIC REALMS

Rolf Gradinger and Bodil A. Bluhm

School of Fisheries and Ocean Sciences, University of Alaska Fairbanks
245 O'Neill Bldg., Fairbanks AK 99775, (907) 474 7407 and (907) 474 6332, Fax (907) 474 7204
E-mail: rgradinger@ims.uaf.edu and bluhm@ims.uaf.edu

Presented by Bodil A. Bluhm.

Traditionally, snow and ice thickness have been considered the critical parameters controlling biological productivity in polar sea ice. In the Arctic, the often high sediment-load within the ice may also be important. We assessed the impact of sediment load on the abundances and composition of near-shore fast ice communities close to Barrow, Alaska in 2002/3. Light in sediment-loaded sea ice (total particle-load 106 g m^{-2}) was reduced by >99% compared to clean ice (6 m^{-2}). Only within the sediment-free ice did we observe a strong ice-algal bloom (max. 330 µgChl a l^{-1}) in the bottom 10 cm in May, while Chl a remained <10 µgChl a l^{-1}in sediment-loaded ice. With increasing ice-algal biomass, the δ^{13}C-ratios of ice-particulate organic matter (POM) and some ice-meiofauna were enriched by up to 10‰ in the sediment-free ice, while no enrichment was observed in dirty ice-POM. Also, the increase in ice-metazoan abundance with season was restricted to clean ice (max. 276,000 individuals m^{-2}). In the pelagic community below, no obvious effect of ice sediment-load was observed. The findings are relevant in the context of increasing sediment-load due to coastal erosion and oil and gas exploration activity and for Arctic-wide production estimates.

Discussion:

Michael Castellini: I have two questions: First, do you know the distribution of the sediment in the ice? And secondly, how much snow would you have to put on clean ice, to make it equivalent to your dirty ice, in terms of impact to the animals?

Bodil Bluhm: The distribution during the time that we were sampling here, the sediment was in the upper 40 centimeters. This can probably vary. The answer, I guess, depends on where in the freezing process the sediment goes into the ice. Now, for our site, even though it was near the surface, it wasn't all the way to the surface. So we couldn't just walk over the ice and actually see it. So the answer is that the sediment distribution is patchy and variable. In our case, it wasn't where the fauna actually was (the fauna concentrate in the bottom 10 cm of the ice).. So otherwise, I could imagine interactions of maybe nutrients or particles being transported to the plants or fauna. But sediment and biota were distinctly separated.

And to answer your second question, the amount of sediment that we had at this dirty ice site, the equivalent in snow layer would be about three meters. Which in that area, correct me if I'm wrong, you don't often have because it is a very wind-blown area. So the snow cover we actually had throughout this study was only some three to seven centimeters. So it's a pretty thick snow layer that you would have to have to come up with the same shading effect the sediment had. There have been a couple of studies on snow, graded snow experiments, and what their effects are. And we were expecting similar responses, only that they really had not been quantified so far for the sediment.

Franz Mueter: I have a somewhat tangential question, I guess. But, you've learned quite a bit about the phytoplankton or primary and secondary productivity in the ice. But most of the upper trophic level species or a lot of them, like birds and Arctic cisco, feed primarily during the open-water season. Do we actually have any idea of what the relative contribution of these ice-associated biota and the open-water production is, and what the link is between the two in terms of either seeding or a direct trophic-level connection?

Bodil Bluhm: Yes and no. I couldn't tell you numbers right now, but the contribution is such that the ice-produced material rains out of the ice eventually. At least the particulate organic matter from the ice then becomes available for the food web underneath, depending on the algal composition. Some algae are a seeding population for the water column production. Some are not; they are just going to rain down to the sea floor where they add organic carbon to whatever lives at the sea floor. What the relative proportions are, we are still trying to figure out, using stable isotope data. These might tell us the proportions at which the zooplankton, for example, was using the ice algae versus the phytoplankton. But there are so many factors now that we didn't anticipate, that we don't have the hard numbers on that yet. Now there are other mechanisms, too. Again I couldn't tell you the numbers, but these under-ice amphipods that I told you about shift food sources, it seems. But they seem to use the sea ice during the bloom as the main food. So they transport some of this material from the ice into the water column. And amphipods, of course, are a primary food source for a number of fish species. So there's a couple of more direct and a couple of more indirect links. But putting that all in numbers I don't think has been done yet.

Bill Streever: That was really interesting to me. I'm glad to see you are doing that and sharing the information in Barrow. And congratulations on making it into the *Arctic Sounder*. I did have a question, and that was, in one of your slides, sort of as a rationale behind this work, you had some real good rationales, obviously something we need to understand. But you also had a bullet in there about the link to industry and potential impacts from sediment associated with exploration. And of course there are a lot of sources of sediment from industry. But I was wondering, in your view, what are key ones that you would be concerned about? What sort of magnitude are we talking about, in terms of potential impacts, and how might that be mitigated?

Bodil Bluhm: That's a good question, and one for which I would probably have to get back to those people that know more about it. We had some debate on that yesterday, on how much sediment comes from these varying sources, from rivers, from coastal erosion, from industrial activities. And I don't know how those numbers play together. I would guess that the exploration activity, overall, probably, but I'm not the expert on this, is more localized in terms of the sediment enrichment effect. So if we look at the Boulder

Patch area that we heard about yesterday, which is in rather close vicinity to some of the exploration activity and that has a very immobile fauna and flora, I would probably expect a stronger impact right there. The sea ice, of course, moves and it's large scale, so I would expect, judging from this year, if we multiply that up to the larger Arctic sea-ice cover, a significant effect. But how that splits into sediment coming from this artificial island or from this river, I don't really know at this point. But I guess, if we had our study on a larger scale, really calibrated biotic effects, and then used the models where there is sediment in the ice, and whether the sediment comes in from local sources, you could probably get a better idea of how relevant the impact would be on the local and the more Arctic-wide scale.

FORAGING ECOLOGY OF COMMON RAVENS (*CORVUS CORAX*) ON ALASKA'S COASTAL PLAIN AND ITS RELATIONSHIP TO OIL AND GAS DEVELOPMENT

Stacia Backensto[1,2] and Abby Powell[1]

[1]Alaska Cooperative Fish and Wildlife Research Unit, 209 Irving I Bldg., University Alaska Fairbanks, AK 99775, (907) 474-5505, ffanp@uaf.edu
[2]Regional Resilience and Adaptation Program, Institute of Arctic Biology, University of Alaska Fairbanks P.O. Box 757000 Fairbanks, AK 99775-7000
(907) 474-7094, ftsab@uaf.edu

Populations of common ravens (*Corvus corax*) on the North Slope of Alaska appear to be increasing where anthropogenic resources are available. The oil fields provide abundant anthropogenic resources in terms of infrastructure and food sources. Winter counts of ravens at the North Slope Borough Prudhoe Bay Landfill appear to be increasing (National Audubon Society 2002). Ravens use infrastructure for nesting and foraging on human food. To assess the potential impact ravens may have as predators of tundra-nesting birds we captured ten breeding adult ravens, attached VHF and satellite transmitters, and tracked their foraging movements during the breeding season. We collected pellet samples and prey remains from nest areas as well as conducted nest observations to evaluate food items brought to the nest. We marked 28 fledglings to determine timing of dispersal as well as juvenile survival. To further investigate seasonal movements, dispersal, and anthropogenic resource use we engaged the community of oil field personnel in an observation program targeting marked birds. Our preliminary findings suggest that breeding adults maintain territories and forage near nesting facilities until late in the chick stage and gradually increase until fledge. Adults shift use of food sources based on availability throughout the breeding season. Juveniles remain with adults and siblings for a period of > 4 weeks after fledge. Breeding adult productivity is high in the oil fields. Industrial infrastructure appears to be important to adult breeding ravens and may contribute to the increasing winter population. Foraging activities are centered on the nest site that suggests predation pressure exerted by ravens on other species may be higher near these facilities.

Literature Cited:

National Audubon Society. 2002. www.audubon.org/bird/cbc/

Discussion:

Kate Wedemeyer: You mentioned the almost 90% survival rate within human areas, and you mentioned that that is found in similar areas around raven territory. Is there any information on the survival with nests that are not near human activity?

Stacia Backensto: The information is a little bit limited in that way. This is a really high survival rate, period. This is just actually the number of fledglings that are getting out of the nest. Relative to other places where the birds are nesting in a more natural area, typical fledgling success rates are about 40 to 60%. Some of the others studies that I mentioned have looked at net survival rate in sites where they're actually nesting on natural structures but they have access to anthropogenic human food sources. Those are still between 60 and 70%. So this is higher overall.

Bill Streever: It's great to see all this information coming out after all these years. Everybody's been worrying about ravens, and all of a sudden we've got more information than we've ever had before. It's great. You mentioned the difference between Kuparuk and Prudhoe. In fact, the area you're calling Prudhoe is actually many different oil fields that were developed in different ways. And then there's this kind of artificial line between the Kuparuk oil field and Prudhoe. It seems like an odd thing to even worry about comparing them. I'm just wondering what your logic is there?

Stacia Backensto: I guess the logic is, it's an easy comparison for us, just from where we worked. But you're right. They're looking at the history of how the technology of those oil fields has progressed on the spatial level is important in understanding infrastructure between both areas. The line is arbitrary; why I've divided Kuparuk and Prudhoe is simply that we had nesting birds that we were successful at trapping and putting transmitters on at Kuparuk. And then in Prudhoe, which that line, again, is like you said (arbitrary). Point taken.

Bill Streever: We'd be happy to talk to you more. But even within your Prudhoe Bay fields, the technologies are very different at different nest sites. In fact, the age range is greater for the development of those fields than it is for Kuparuk versus the actual Prudhoe Bay field.

Stacia Backensto: And I think that is a necessary important step to further understand this range of infrastructure. I would like to emphasize, this is my gross interpretation of infrastructure right now. But we're hoping through time to really polish that description and the understanding of what infrastructure is and it's importance to ravens.

Tom Newbury: I have a question about subsidized predators and natural predators. When a subsidized predator moves into an area, does it displace the natural predator or does the subsidy it gets allow it to use a niche that wouldn't otherwise be filled? In other words, does it add a species or does it displace a natural predator on small mammals? Things like skuas. They prey on small mammals. When a raven moves in, when it's subsidized and moves in, does it displace the skua?

Stacia Backensto: That's a really good question that I don't have an answer for. There might be some competitive exclusion there between ravens and other predators. Even though we're calling the raven a subsidized predator in this system, the raven is also a natural predator in the Arctic. And it's important to distinguish, to identify in that discussion that ravens are present in the Arctic. They have been in the Arctic before the oil fields. What we think we're seeing now is a redistribution of raven populations in the Arctic. It's likely that where there's a high concentration of breeding ravens, that they might displace other natural predators. But we do see those predators in the oil fields, around those raven nest sites. What is really important to breeding ravens, however, is other breeding ravens. They're very territorial within their own species, but they're probably more tolerant of other predators being in their territory.

ANALYSIS OF VARIATION IN ABUNDANCE OF ARCTIC CISCO IN THE COLVILLE RIVER: ANALYSIS OF PATTERNS IN EXISTING DATA

Stephen M. Murphy[1], Franz J. Mueter[2], Stephen R. Braund[3],
Lawrence J. Moulton[4], and Robert H. Day[1]

[1]ABR, Inc., P.O. Box 80410, Fairbanks, AK 99708, (907) 455-6777, E-mail: smurphy@abrinc.com.;
[2] Sigma Plus, 697 Fordham Drive, Fairbanks, AK, 99709, (907) 479-8815, E-mail: fmueter@alaska.net;
[3] Stephen R. Braund & Assoc., P.O. Box 1480 Anchorage, AK 99510, (907) 276-8222
Email: srba@alaska.net;
[4] MJM Research, 1012 Shoreland Drive, Lopez Island, WA 98261, (206) 842-8654
E-mail: lmoulton@rockisland.com

Presented by Dr. Franz Mueter in Anchorage and by Stephen Braund in Barrow.

Arctic cisco (*Coregonus autumnalis*) are an important subsistence resource for residents of the North Slope of Alaska. Low harvest rates on the Colville River subsistence fishery in several recent years have prompted MMS to sponsor a study that examines available data on Arctic cisco biology and natural and anthropogenic factors that affect the abundance of Arctic cisco available for harvest. In addition to analyzing long-term data sets from scientific studies that have been conducted on Arctic cisco and examining regional data sets on weather and oceanographic conditions that may be influencing key life history events that take place in the Beaufort Sea and Colville River, this study will engage a Panel of Local Experts to help guide the analytical work and interpretation of results. A social networking approach will be used to select a panel from the residents of Nuiqsut. Input from the Panel will be important both for identifying the appropriate data sets for use in the analyses and for deriving alternate hypotheses to be tested in the data exploration and analytical phases of this study. Hence, traditional knowledge will be used as more than just anecdotal information or a as qualitative variable, but rather will form the basis for many of the analyses the scientific team will conduct. Communication with the Panel will be maintained throughout the life of the study, and frequent meetings will be held in Nuiqsut. The Kuukpik Subsistence Oversight Panel of Nuiqsut is a key team member that will help facilitate meetings with the Panel and will assist the Panel with reporting obligations.

Once the panel is selected and relevant data sets are identified and acquired, the study team will use a multivariate approach to explore relationships among existing data sets, and statistical models will be constructed to identify potential effects of the natural and human environment on Arctic cisco populations. To reduce the chances of identifying spurious relationships, variables for these models will be carefully selected *a priori* and will be used to test specific hypotheses. These hypotheses will be developed based on previous research, combined with input from the Panel of Local Experts. Through exploratory analyses, statistical modeling, sensitivity analyses, and input from the Panel of Local Experts, this study will examine and identify the natural and human factors that affect variability in the Arctic cisco population available for harvest by North Slope residents. The study also will identify future research topics and data needs.

Discussion:

Cleve Cowles: I was interested in your graphic showing the coastal transport. Over near the mouth of the Mackenzie, you had a very discrete line, which from a conceptual standpoint makes it look like a fairly narrow corridor for all fish, all ciscoes. Is that verified by north-south transect studies and for young-of-the-year fish?

Franz Mueter: Well, this is a sketch of current understanding. There has been some sampling along the way. There's been some sampling up in the Mackenzie Delta. And I have to say I'm not all that familiar with all those studies yet. So, there's actually no doubt that a lot of the Arctic cisco may go the other direction as well, off of Canada. There are some uncertainties about Arctic cisco coming from the Barrow direction.

Cleve Cowles: That's kind of what I was going to ask. Because my conceptual model is of the Mackenzie emptying into the Beaufort Sea and the plumes extend quite far offshore. You can see how they break off and spiral, when you see the ice patterns, or at least the surface representation of those plumes. It's not unlikely then that young-of-the-year fish are actually out farther offshore and are transported in multiple directions. Then they may be blown across and come up against the shoreline through some processes, farther to the west.

Franz Mueter: So they would completely bypass Prudhoe Bay, is what you are saying?

Cleve Cowles: Well, I'm just saying that they wouldn't necessarily follow that discrete blue line on your graphic.

Franz Mueter: No, this is definitely just a sketch of what we think is going on. It's unlikely that they do go far offshore because they do avoid high salinities.

Cleve Cowles: I'm impressed with the interplay between the scientific and non-scientific community. When you present findings or sketches like this, is this the nature of the presentation to the non-scientific community? And are they aware of the conceptual model that I was just kind of trying to run through.

Franz Mueter: Well, we haven't done that yet. The first meeting is scheduled later this month, which will be basically devoted to just choosing a panel of experts there. And the follow-up meeting to that, I will be going down there. And the way we see it right now is that we will take the results from that 2003 meeting, what we can glean from the literature, what's known so far or at least our understanding of what we know so far, and present it in non-technical terms to the local experts. Then we'll get feed-back and additional input and ideas of other factors that we didn't consider or didn't pick up from previous work.

Cleve Cowles: Thanks. That clarifies it. I appreciate that very much. I think it would be important that our conceptual models are not too defined when we don't have that kind of information about the migration over to the east of there.

Franz Mueter: Right. There is definitely a very crude sketch.

Lee Benner: As you pointed out, we've been doing studies on Arctic cisco for a number of years. And over that time, I've heard that one of things that has been noticed is that the fish are thinner than usual. And you just mentioned it again. I'm curious. What or when is the "usual" that is being referred to?

Franz Mueter: Well, the only times that I've come across it is in the reports from some previous meetings. And that was mostly based on the fishermen in the village who repeatedly said that it looks like, in recent years, the fish have been skinnier than they used to be. There is data available from the fishery on size and weight, as well as from the Prudhoe Bay area on size, weight and age. So you could look at weight at age. Larry Moulton has looked at that previously and, for the years for which he looked at the time, he found quite a lot of variability in weight at age, or at a given size. But not any evidence of a decline. But I'm just kind of speculating at this point. I have not looked at the data yet, but there is data available to get at that, at least going back to 1985. I can't answer that question yet, but hopefully we will be able to give them what I know about what's available.

Bill Streever: You mentioned the commercial fishery briefly. I wonder if Jim Helmericks is involved in some of these briefings you are doing in the village? Or if you intend to brief him separately, or how that's going to work, as one of your key stakeholders?

Franz Mueter: Well, actually I don't know at this point. He was probably aware of it because Larry Moulton has worked with him in the past. And I will keep that in mind. We will try to make sure that we at least inform them of what we are up to.

Discussion from the Barrow IUM:

Doreen Lampe: Is there any qaaktaq (Arctic cisco) elsewhere in the world? Are there some in Russia?

Steve Braund: I am not sure on that side. At the Anchorage ITM, there were people from Tuktoyaktuk Harbor, Canada and Norm Snow from Inuvik, Canada. They said there is a substantial Arctic cisco harvested in Tuktoyaktuk Harbor. They call it herring. He said that the cisco go at least 800 miles to the east. They go at least as far as the eastern Arctic.

Doreen Lampe: Is there any indication that they go to the west of Barrow? I was curious because it is in a major development area.

Steve Braund: Good question. I don't know the answer to that. Craig?

Craig George: The genetic evidence says that Arctic cisco probably come from Canada. That is sort of the center of distribution. There are some really big ones over there, also. When you get farther west along the coast, you get into the Bering cisco out of the Yukon drainage. As you go west, you get almost all Bering-type cisco. If you go east, and then into Arctic Canada, it is all the arctic type which are a different species. But that is a good question.

I think that it is great that this study is finally happening. One of the key questions is what happens to the return spawners? In other words, the adult fish from the Colville, that mature and then leave. As you know, you almost never catch a qaaktaq with ripe eggs. They are very rare. Occasionally you see them but almost all of those take off for the Mackenzie. Or that is the thinking. So the question is: "What happens to those and are their progeny the ones that are coming back to the west?" There was some genetic evidence that the Colville River Arctic cisco are mainly from a couple of drainages on the Mackenzie, like the Arctic Red River and some that were farthest down river. So it is not like a mix of all of them. There might be specific drainages that make it there.

But the question is if we fish hard in the Colville, will it have an effect on the recruitment later? I don't think that has ever been answered. The assumption is that there isn't. But I don't know if that was ever established.

The other thing is the effect of causeways on fish. For the Arctic cisco, the evidence showed it wasn't important. The Science Advisory Committee for the Borough concluded that after a lot of years. But for other less saline tolerant species, like least cisco or humpback whitefish, it was a problem.

But I am glad that someone is going to revisit that and make sure that our conclusions were correct: that those young-of-the-year fish are going around the causeways.

LOCATING OVERWINTERING FISH HABITAT
SAGAVANIRKTOK AND COLVILLE RIVERS/BEAUFORT SEA

Claude Duguay[1], Richard Brown[2], Peter Doucette[3], Larry Moulton[4], and Robert Mueller[2]

[1] Geophysical Institute, University of Alaska Fairbanks
903 Koyukuk Dr., P.O. Box 757320, Fairbanks, AK 99775–7320
(907) 474-6832, Fax (907) 474-7290, E-mail: claude.duguay@gi.alaska.edu
[2] Battelle/PNNL, P.O. Box 999, MS K6-85, Richland, WA 99352
(509) 376-5002, Fax (509) 372-3515, E-Mail: rich.brown@pnl.gov, robert.mueller@pnl.gov
[3] Battelle/PNNL, 1529 W. Sequim Bay Rd., Sequim, WA 98382
(360) 681-3698, Fax (360) 681-3699, E-mail: peter.doucette@pnl.gov
[4] MJM Consulting, 1012 Shoreline Dr., Lopez Island, WA 98261
(360) 468-4821, E-mail: lmoulton@rockisland.com

In northern climates, winter is a critical time of year for fish survival. Unlike marine fish, many of which form anti-freeze proteins in winter to enable them to live in sub-zero marine waters, freshwater fish have no mechanism to avoid freezing. Freshwater areas can only dip slightly below freezing during brief supercooling events; however, marine waters can reach temperatures as low as -1.9°C. This means anadromous fish (i.e., fish that spawn in freshwater and live most of their lives in saltwater) must leave marine waters to dwell in overwintering habitats influenced by fresh water. However, the amount of fresh water habitat is often drastically reduced by a curtailment in flows and by formation of both surface and subsurface river ice. Salmonids typically react to this limitation of overwintering habitat by squeezing into pockets of suitable habitats. Fish often form large aggregations in these limited habitats. In Arctic climates, this limitation of habitats is even more extreme since large parts of rivers freeze completely to the bottom.

In ice-covered rivers, fish typically prefer deep areas or locations influenced by groundwater; in these locations they often use surface ice, woody debris, or substrate as cover. Since large numbers of fish may be squeezed into a relatively small amount of space, protection of these areas is key. Also, areas that have deep water during open water periods may not necessarily provide good habitat during winter due to the formation of large subsurface ice formations called hanging dams, which can fill large parts of pools or even entire river reaches.

Due to ice cover in northern climates, locating overwintering areas can be very challenging. Radio-telemetry is most often used to identify the overwintering areas of fish where ice cover makes other techniques such as snorkeling impossible. However, radio-telemetry projects can be expensive if they require covering large spatial areas and multiple species of fish. Also extensive use of helicopters and fixed wing aircraft can be cost-prohibitive and dangerous under poor weather conditions. Spaceborne synthetic aperture radar (SAR) provides a means to look at the problem of fish overwintering habitat from a broader perspective.

Recent investigations have shown the potential of SAR imagery for locating areas of floating and grounded (frozen to the bottom) ice on shallow lakes on the North Slope of Alaska and the Hudson Bay Lowland, Canada. One objective of this study is to determine whether the approaches developed in these studies can be extended to locate such areas on rivers (and connected lakes) of the North Slope of Alaska. Of particular interest are the areas of floating ice, which are the most probable overwintering locations for anadromous fish in low gradient areas of the Arctic coastal plain. A preliminary assessment of the approach was conducted in an area near the mouth of the Sagavanirktok River. Field observations were made coincident with the acquisition of Advanced SAR (ASAR) Alternating Polarization (AP) images from the European Envisat satellite in April 2004. Results show that SAR offers a promising means for mapping potential fish overwintering habitat locations on rivers and lakes of the North Slope of Alaska. Further validation and refinement of the approach is, however, needed before moving into operational use on the Sagavanirktok and Colville rivers, as well as other Arctic rivers and lakes.

Discussion:

John Petterson: Do you see any trend on the interannual variability?

Claude Duguay: I can't really answer that question since we haven't examined this yet. However, the probability map we produced from several years of data provides a good idea of the normal ice conditions. This map can be compared to images of individual years to get a sense of the interannual variability. This certainly merits closer examination.

John Petterson: Your 1993 showed very little, and your 2003 showed a great deal.

Claude Duguay: Yes, a lot of floating ice in 2003.

John Petterson: You don't see a trend?

Claude Duguay: Again, I can't give you a straight answer right now. But I know, looking at the time series of images, that sometimes three or four years in a row you get a lot of floating ice, and then you have two years with more grounded ice. That's an aspect we have to look at in the future. Another aspect we need to examine is the variations within a year. That is looking at time-sequence images acquired from the beginning of ice formation towards later in the winter and seeing how this evolves through time on a given year, and then between years.

Vera Alexander: I am just a little curious about this ice-water interface and its effects on your images. I note from my years working up in the Arctic, that very often, especially in spring, when you drill a hole in a lake, the water will come spurting out or it will go roaring in. Most often it will go roaring into the hole and drain the whole surface of the lake. That leaves a gap between the ice and the water. Does this have any effect?

Claude Duguay: Well, you probably have a similar effect. Because if you do have some air between the ice and water, the radar signal goes through the ice and through the air. And then when it hits the water, there will be some return and some interactions with the ice cover. However, during springtime you can have wet conditions on the ice surface, so that a large portion of the radar signal is absorbed. So the approach I described works well, of course, in the winter period. But as soon as you get into the melt period, then you get a lot of effects due to the presence of water in the snow pack at the top of the ice or ponding of water on top of the ice surface.

Franz Mueter: I think it is a fascinating tool. I wasn't aware that satellite imagery could do that and tell you those sorts of things. But from an Arctic cisco perspective, if you are an Arctic cisco trying to overwinter in the Colville, what you are concerned about is, obviously, pockets of open water. But you don't want to get stuck there because you may run out of oxygen or you may want to be able to move downstream to go into areas that are your preferred habitats. With this tool, do you think you can actually tell with the kind of spatial resolution that you have, whether these pockets do have a connection to the Delta or not?

Claude Duguay: You could monitor the pockets as well, using radar. But if I wished to do that, I would look at time series from the beginning of ice formation through the winter. Because the danger of doing it only in April, for example, is that some areas are frozen to the beds. And open water areas can have very similar signatures, very similar gray levels. So, I would probably try to track this through the winter period before the ice started to freeze to the bottom, so as to be able to really pick those up.

Discussion from the Barrow IUM:

Craig George: It looks like you are not showing water offshore of deltas. That was one of the questions that some local people and I had. Do Arctic cisco winter offshore of the deltas and no one knows? It would be quite interesting if you could identify freshwater areas offshore.

Claude Duguay: The radar images cover some of the offshore areas as well. However, in the slide I showed we masked that section.

Craig George: In the area near Barrow you showed, all those white areas match quite nicely the areas where local people fish in the winter.

Claude Duguay: As I said, it is interesting for me, coming from the physical side; I was totally unaware of the potential of this technique.

Doreen Lampe: Is this technique used elsewhere to determine fish populations?

Claude Duguay: Not that I am aware of. The Canadian Ice Service uses radar images to determine ice conditions for navigation purposes in the Arctic. The Radarsat satellite that I mentioned is a Canadian satellite. The main purpose of the mission is to monitor ice conditions and to relay that information to ships in the Arctic. The National Ice Center in the U.S. works in collaboration with the Canadian Ice Service for some ice monitoring, on the Great Lakes I believe. To my knowledge there has been very little use of that in real world applications, from an operational sense.

Craig George: A lot of the high-resolution maps that we have for the whaling community are the Radarsat images.

Claude Duguay: There is starting to be more interest. I saw a presentation at the remote sensing conference in Anchorage last September, where they were using some of these radar images to try to find areas where seals would pop up in open water areas of the sea ice in the Arctic Ocean. There is more and more interest in using this technology for habitat studies.

Craig George: Is all the imagery coming from Canada?

Claude Duguay: No. The Alaska Satellite Facility (ASF) receives images from the European satellite ERS-2 and ERS-1 prior to that, as well at the Canadian Radarsat-1 satellite. However, ASF is not receiving Advanced SAR images from the Envisat satellite. However, I have a project approved by the European Space Agency which gives me access to ASAR images.

THE COASTAL MARINE INSTITUTE AT THE UNIVERSITY OF ALASKA FAIRBANKS: AN OVERVIEW OF CMI AND SYNOPSES OF TWO RECENTLY APPROVED CMI STUDIES

Vera Alexander, Ph.D.

Coastal Marine Institute, School of Fisheries and Ocean Sciences
University of Alaska Fairbanks, P.O. Box 757220, Fairbanks, AK 99775
(907) 474-5071, Fax (907) 474-7386

The Coastal Marine Institute was created in 1993 by a cooperative agreement between the University of Alaska and the U.S. Department of the Interior Minerals Management Service (MMS) to study coastal topics associated with the development of natural gas, oil, and minerals in Alaska's outer continental shelf (OCS). All CMI funded projects address one of the following current framework issues:

1. Scientific studies for better understanding marine, coastal, or human environments affected or potentially affected by offshore oil and gas or other mineral exploration and extraction on the OCS
2. Modeling studies of environmental, social, economic, or cultural processes related to OCS gas and oil activities in order to improve scientific predictive capabilities
3. Experimental scientific studies for better understanding of environmental processes or the causes and effects of OCS activities
4. Projects which design or establish mechanisms or protocols for sharing of data or scientific information regarding marine or coastal resources or human activities to support prudent management of oil and gas and marine mineral resources
5. Synthesis studies of scientific environmental or socioeconomic information relevant to the OCS gas and oil program.

CMI projects are diverse in scope, focus, and geographic location. Some examples of recent projects include studies of sediment samples in Shelikof Strait, analyses of King Eider molting areas and migrations, explorations into the foraging ecology of common ravens on the Arctic Coastal Plain, studies of water and ice dynamics in Cook Inlet, and investigations into Beaufort Sea ice.

"Pre-Migratory movements and Physiology of Shorebirds Staging on Alaska's North Slope" by Audrey R. Taylor, Abby N. Powell, Richard B. Lanctot, and Tony D. Williams is important because proposed expansion of oil and gas development on the North Slope may pose a threat to staging shorebirds and their habitat. Study objectives include expanding current knowledge of shorebird species composition on Alaska's North Slope, tracking shorebird tenure time at specific staging sites, and assessing the importance and quality of different staging sites. Study methods include painting and banding individual birds and bleeding birds to analyze triglyceride blood levels. Preliminary results for the 2004 field season include sighting a variety of shorebird species, capturing and bleeding 204 individual shorebirds, resighting 158 birds, and noting the various tenure times for different species. The study plan for 2005 includes slope-wide aerial surveys to determine species composition and distribution, using radio telemetry to analyze bird staging patterns, and blood testing individual birds to determine if physiology is indicative of staging site quality.

"Evaluating a Potential Relict Arctic Invertebrate and Algal Community on the West Side of Cook Inlet" by Susan Saupe, Nora Foster, and Dennis Lees is currently underway. The study proposes to expand current knowledge of species composition of intertidal and subtidal benthic assemblages on the west side of Cook Inlet and evaluate the degree of geographic isolation for each potential relict Arctic species by reviewing previous studies conducted in other areas. Study methods include conducting taxonomic analyses of invertebrates and algae, assessing geographic isolation of different species by reviewing past and current studies, and comparing species found in the study area with species recorded in other areas of Cook Inlet. This project is still in its beginning stages but taxonomic analysis of some specimens is already underway.

For more information about the Coastal Marine Institute, please visit
http://www.sfos.uaf.edu/cmi/.

No Discussion.

ONGOING PROJECTS OF THE DEPARTMENT OF WILDLIFE MANAGEMENT, NORTH SLOPE BOROUGH

Mr. Craig George

Department of Wildlife Management, North Slope Borough
P.O. Box 69, Barrow, AK 99723
(907) 852-0350, Fax (907) 852-0351, E-mail: Craig.George@north-slope.org

---

Presented by Dr. Robert Suydam in Anchorage and Craig George in Barrow.

The North Slope Borough (NSB) extends from the Canadian Border to the Chukchi Sea and more or less from the divide in the Brooks Range up to the Beaufort Sea. At about 89,000 square miles, it is the largest municipality in the U.S., yet with a very low population density. It includes eight villages, as well as the oil fields at Prudhoe Bay, Kuparuk, and Alpine. The Department of Wildlife Management (DWM) of the North Slope Borough was formed in the early 1980s. The Department's original mission was to primarily to conduct bowhead whale research. More recently, it has expanded to facilitate sustainable harvest of all subsistence species such as bowheads, eiders, fish, or other wildlife, and to monitor the health of wildlife populations through research. The unique aspect of the Department is the integration of western science and traditional knowledge, of which the bowhead program is a good example. The Borough supports a staff of scientists, subsistence specialists, and research assistants, as well as administrative and support personnel. Recently the Borough's budget has been cut, and we have been encouraged to seek grant funds. Currently we have about 30 active grants from various funding sources, including the National Oceanic and Atmospheric Administration (NOAA), the Bureau of Land Management (BLM), and U.S. Fish and Wildlife Service (USFWS). We've also had a few projects supported by MMS through Coastal Marine Institute (CMI), and now the bulk of our funding comes through NPR-A impact funds through the State of Alaska.

Bowhead and Beluga Whale Research

National Marine Fisheries Service (NMFS) started the bowhead whale research, primarily on abundance surveys and photo identification, in the 1970s. Since the early 1980s the DWM has taken on the role of conducting many of these studies. In the more than 25 years of Department studies, a large amount of information on bowhead whales has been produced. The current population estimate is about 10,500 animals, and the stock appears to be increasing at about 3 to 4% per year. Much of the information that we gather is presented and reviewed at the International Whaling Commission (IWC). The IWC held and

"In-Depth Assessment" of bowhead whales in 2004 with 50 papers presented, and another one is planned for 2007 when the 5-year block quota is re-evaluated. Currently the most important issue regarding bowheads at the IWC is stock structure, and is currently our main emphasis; however other research is on going. We are conducting genetics and physiology work, in collaboration with other researchers. We're working on humane killing issues by working with the AEWC on weapons improvement. In coming years we hope to be working with MMS and the Alaska Department of Fish and Game (ADF&G) on satellite tagging. Bowhead age analysis is continuing. Evidence that these whales are long lived (150 to 200 years) comes from both aspartic acid racemization studies and the estimated age of spear points found in recently harvested whales.

The Department is also investigating beluga whales and their habitat uses in Alaska. Tagging studies have revealed that they range far to the north, even into regions with apparently complete ice cover.

Caribou Research

Since 1990, the Department has conducted a caribou research program, in conjunction with ADF&G and BLM, which is focused on the distribution and movement of caribou from the Teshekpuk Lake herd. The study of satellite-collared caribou has provided a better understanding of habitat use and selection by the herd for calving, summer feeding/insect relief, and wintering areas. Future work will focus on plant-animal interactions, foraging effects on tundra, and evaluating the effects of seismic activity on caribou distribution. This information is important for making wise decisions about exploration and development, especially in the NPR-A area.

Bird Studies

A King Eider project was funded through CMI, with support from the Borough and BLM, as well as other sources. We are also working with USFWS in understanding breeding biology of Steller's Eiders, Black Brandt, and snow geese, and helping with conservation planning for Steller's Eiders, looking at King and Common Eider migration past Point Barrow, and satellite-tagging glaucous gulls.

Fisheries Research

In our fisheries research, we have recently been tracking movements of various fish within NPR-A and assessing basic fish distribution and abundance. We are also conducting contaminant research focusing on hydrocarbons and PAHs. A goal of the contaminants is to collect baseline data on hydrocarbons prior to large-scale oil and gas activity. We have been collecting traditional knowledge from the experienced hunters and fishers in Barrow; and a related effort will be conveying this complex information to the local people of the North Slope.

Subsistence Studies

An important part of the Department's work is to document subsistence harvest and the areas that are used for subsistence, through baseline data collected for each of the North Slope communities.

We also communicate and collaborate with industry for environmental studies and decisions, help guide oil and gas leasing, exploration and development, look at EISs, guide lease sales, and provide guidance for decisions that agencies make about lease sales. NSB's Fish and Game Management Committee provides opportunities for agencies, universities, and industry to discuss various issues with North Slope community representatives. This Committee serves as the advisory committee to the Alaska Migratory Bird Co-Management Council, as well as to the ADF&G.

Discussion:

Ben Greene: The one feature of northern latitudes that is gaining attention in academic, scientific circles, as well as in the general media and general awareness in the public, is global climatic change. It just occurred to me that the North Slope Borough and the scientific advisors and biologists working for the Borough are in a very central position to provide input, to lend some of your knowledge to global climatic change studies. And I'm wondering if you've been putting your efforts in that direction as well?

Robert Suydam: Thank you for the question. We are, of course, incredibly concerned about climate change. We are, I agree, in a really good position to help answer some of the questions and to help pose some of the questions even. And I think we are in that position because of the data sets that we have, because of the history of our department, how long we've been there. But probably most importantly, is our relationship with the hunters. The traditional knowledge typically tells us so much more, at least in the sort term, or the immediate, than science. The people that have been living up here have heard stories from their grandparents and parents, and have lived on the land for their entire lives. They have seen a lot of changes in their lives. So helping to understand that and helping to put some of that down is definitely something that we're interested in doing. We've been involved in a couple different National Science Foundation (NSF) projects to help look at some of those questions. We're certainly interested in those kinds of issues from a research and a management perspective. One example is that when we count bowhead whales, we do it from the ice edge. We go out in springtime at Barrow, set up a camp, set up a perch, put hydrophones in the water, and listen and watch for bowheads. But with changes in ice conditions, it means it's much more difficult for us to do that. It's much more dangerous, or the conditions just aren't suitable for us to be out there counting. It means we may have to change how we count bowheads. So there are issues like that, which we're definitely interested in and concerned with. One of the things that I didn't put in this talk is that we've been really involved in working with the Barrow Arctic Science Consortium, which is providing a lot of logistical support for NSF-sponsored projects in Barrow. And a new research facility is about to be built in Barrow, and so we're very supportive of that. The title of that research facility is the Barrow Arctic Climate Change Research Facility. The amount of science that will be going on in Barrow is going to increase dramatically, is increasing dramatically.

Discussion from the Barrow IUM:

Arnold Brower, Jr.: Do the variations on the isotope chart mean anything?

Craig George: The way Don Schell interpreted it, and I think he is right, is that the graph shows feeding in the Beaufort Sea, and then feeding the Bering. So these are annual migrations. From oceanographic work we now know that the Bering signal is mostly from the krill coming up from the Bering Sea. Whereas, over to the east, the signal is from copepods near Kaktovik and farther. But you can get that Bering signal starting at Barrow. The food here looks isotopically like Bering Sea. So Don Schell always said that there is winter feeding. But I think that there is more and more evidence that it is not winter feeding but fall feeding, where they are picking up the Bering signal. But that is sort of an ongoing study.

Arnold Brower, Jr.: If there is 100% ice cover, how do you track the belugas?

Craig George: They have to come to the surface. Where there is 10/10ths ice, there are always cracks. But if you look at the ice maps, there are no big polynas or open water areas. The belugas are in some extraordinarily heavy ice. Some of the belugas that were tagged in the Mackenzie Gulf did the same thing. They came all the way from Canada and charged up 500 miles into the pack ice. From the pressure sensors on the tags, they know they made V-shaped dives of about a half a mile or more, 3000 feet or more. They wonder if they are going down to feed, then looking for the light, etc., and coming up to that opening, then diving down again and repeating the process.

I think when we tag bowheads; we'll find that everything we know is wrong from a scientific sense. I think that the Iñupiat model of a more labile distribution is going to hold up. A lot of the old timers have told us for years that there are bowheads that summer in the pack ice. Some of the aerial surveys have shown a few, but I bet we'll find more than we realize. There is some evidence of this; when population surveys were done in Canada, they could only come up with half of the whales that we see here. So they are somewhere.

George Olemaun: You mentioned that there are different groups that come up. Does that have anything to do with their age?

Craig George: That is a good question. Again, it is the question of bowhead stocks. The jury is not out on that. Actually it is interesting that you mention age because one of the stronger explanations of some of the genetic differences that are being seen, (again no one is calling them stocks yet), is that these extremely old animals, as a group, may have different genetic traits than the young do now, just due to selective breeding through the years. Actually, we have seen genetic differences in whales of different ages. I guess a good analogy would be your great-great grandparents as a group might have different traits that the young kids around town today. So we are still working on that with the NMFS's Southwest Fisheries Lab in La Jolla, California. That is a good point.

George Olemaun: You mentioned using traditional knowledge, how is that used in your studies?

Craig George: Because our department is half Iñupiat, I like to think that traditional knowledge is integrated into almost everything that we do. We try and keep our feet on the ground in terms of making sure that the work we do has some basis in what local people have observed. And then, again, one of the best things that the community can do, when we get our results, is to question them. We talk with the community and ask if jour results make sense: "This is what we are seeing. We see whales migrating under 100% ice. Does this make sense? Hunters respond, "Sure it makes sense, we've seen the same thing." Or maybe they haven't. So that is the next step. It is one thing to integrate it initially. But I think it is really important, just as in any good scientific project or approach to a question, to question the results. And to keep questioning them to make sure that they make sense with all of the observations you make. If there is a disconnect, then you figure out why. That is how the scientific process works.

Charlie Hopson: I have a cabin on a river near the Teshekpuk. Two years ago we talked about two stocks of whitefish. We weren't sure if they were one stock or two. Have you finished that study you were going to do about the whitefish that go up the Ikpikpuk, Mayoriak, and Teshekpuk that they might be connected with the fish that go up to Kukpuk (Colville). I know that the Kukpuk whitefish are different.

Craig George: It is ongoing.

Charlie Hopson: We need to keep studying that in case something happens in one of the rivers. Are we going to be killing off all of the fish that go up to different rivers? We talked about that two years ago, one year ago; how far along are you?

Craig George: Charlie brings up a question about stocks of broad whitefish. I think that there are going to be different groups. The fish that were tagged here looked like they were moving through the Ikpikpuk-Chipp System. This may be a common breeding stock. This summer we are going to tag fish in the Keolak River drainage. But just so you know, none of the Colville River fish have been seen or recaptured in this area. The other place that we need to study is in the Meade. So this summer we want to tag some fish in the Meade river system to see if they are overlapping with the Ikpikpuk fish.

Charlie Hopson: So you are saying that you actually don't know what these fish are. So I think we better get going and do this study. Industry is among us. It is taking too long. I don't want you beating around the bush and telling me that it is going to be done. We said that two years ago. MMS is here; they have a lot of money. Let's get these studies done before it is too late.

Craig George: That is a good point. Let's get it done.

Protected Species

DEMOGRAPHY AND BEHAVIOR OF POLAR BEARS FEEDING ON STRANDED MARINE MAMMAL CARCASSES

Susanne Miller

Marine Mammals Management, U. S. Fish and Wildlife Service
1011 E. Tudor Road, Anchorage, AK 99503
(907) 786-3828, Fax (907) 786-3816, Email: Susanne_Miller@fws.gov

In 2002-2004, the U.S. Fish and Wildlife Service conducted a study on polar bears feeding on bowhead whale carcasses at Barter and Cross islands, Alaska. The purpose of the study was to determine the number, age/sex composition, behavior, and habitat use of polar bears using these feeding sites during the fall open water period prior to freeze-up. In recent years, the number of polar bears using coastal habitat in the Beaufort Sea region has increased; reasons for the increase are unknown but may be related to the presence of subsistence-harvested bowhead whale remains, environmental, or other factors. Monitoring bears using the near shore environment helps wildlife biologists and managers identify and conserve important habitat areas, as well as minimize potential bear-human conflicts.

Systematic observations were conducted in September/October, 2002-2004 at Barter and Cross islands. Scan sampling methods were used to determine number, age, and sex of polar bears in the study areas; focal animal sampling of randomly selected cohorts was used to determine time-activity budgets (behavior).

Data was collected during 1,231 hours of observations, comprised of 4,733 scans and 925 focal samples. Findings confirm that relatively high densities of polar bears occur on Barter and Cross islands during fall months, compared to other coastal areas in the Beaufort Sea region. All age/sex classes of polar bears (adults, family groups, sub-adults, single bears of unknown age/sex) were observed using feeding sites at both Barter and Cross islands. Overall, laying, feeding, and walking constituted the highest proportion of observed behaviors. Habitat types used by polar bears included mainland, barrier island, and marine waters; ice habitat was not present in the study areas during the study period. Specific details regarding polar bear demography, temporal use, and behavior will be presented pending final analyses.

Discussion:

Mike Castellini: Did you have grizzly bears feeding at both Barter and Cross islands?

Susanne Miller: No. They were just at Barter Island and just at the feeding site. We never saw brown bears out on Bernard Spit either.

Charles Monnett: You mentioned that the reason there were more bears possibly at Barter Island was because the ice was in closer to shore there, and that they move from east to west. I'm just remembering back a few years when there were a lot of bears at Barrow because of the whale carcasses that were left on the beach during the summer. What was the story there? What was the timing and where did those bears come from?

Susanne Miller: I remember it was late August, early September. Typically you don't see the large aggregations in Barrow until later in the season. So, I don't know, it is probably related to the distance of the pack ice from shore. What we are seeing from some of our data is that the farther the ice is from shore, the more bears there tend to be on land. And I don't know if that's because they're swimming all the way from the pack ice edge, or they're accessing land farther east and then walking west. We don't really understand that fully. (Author's note: In 2002 large aggregations at Barrow were a result of pack ice blowing in close to shore and depositing a large number of bears near Barrow, then rapidly retreating from shore, essentially leaving the bears stranded there. These bears were most likely from the

Bering/Chukchi seas population of polar bears, versus the Beaufort Sea population bears using Cross and Barter islands.)

Charles Monnett: So there could be bears coming directly ashore then in the far west?

Susanne Miller: Yes. That could be happening. The ice habitat is so dynamic.

Lee Benner: You made the comment that there are more bears being seen on shore than before. I think that's what you said. And then you were looking at where they were feeding. And I believe these are traditional sites for the harvesting of captured whales. So it's not clear to me if these harvesting sites have been there for years and years. Are you saying that people were not seeing bears there before but now they are? Or they're seeing more bears? I'm missing the connection here.

Susanne Miller: I think that any time that you have a marine mammal carcass like a whale on shore, whether it's subsistence harvested or died of natural causes, the likelihood of seeing large numbers of bears during that time of year is good. They have a very good sense of smell and obviously are going to be attracted to that as a food source. The reason that we chose Barter Island and Cross Island is because bowhead whales are reliably and consistently harvested there for subsistence purposes. So we knew if we set up our study in those locations that there was a very good chance that bears would be there because there would be bowhead remains would be there. One of the reasons why we want to do the traditional knowledge study is to try to determine is to how long that has been going on. It's my understanding that both Cross Island and Barter Island have been used traditionally for hundreds of years for whaling, but that the phenomena of there reliably (consistently) being that whale meat year after year has only been going on since maybe the 1970s when Kaktovik and Nuiqsut became incorporated under ANILCA as villages. So the traditional use is there, but the regular fall whaling at those places is a more recent phenomenon.

POLAR BEAR POPULATION MONITORING WORKSHOP

Craig Perham

Marine Mammal Management, USFWS
1011 E. Tudor Road. Anchorage, AK 99503
(907) 786-3810, Fax (907) 786-3816, Email: craig_perham@fws.gov

---

On September 3-5, 2003, the U.S. Fish and Wildlife Service (FWS) sponsored a workshop in Anchorage, Alaska. The goal of this meeting was to identify components for development of a comprehensive, long-term monitoring program for polar bears in relation to the oil and gas industry activities in Alaska. This workshop was the initial effort to improve current data collection methods and design an effective monitoring strategy that will provide information to help reduce bear/human interactions, protect polar bear habitat, and more accurately assess potential effects of oil and gas on the Southern Beaufort Sea polar bear stock. Potential oil and gas industry impacts on polar bears which were discussed during the workshop included: habitat alteration, chemical contamination, attraction and preclusion of areas, oil spills, industrial noise, and polar bear interactions with humans. Based on the information discussed, the monitoring workshop identified guidelines for the next 10 years necessary to evaluate the status and trends of polar bears in Alaska.

Discussion:

Bill Streever: That was a great summary. You mentioned that the first special regulations were issued in November 1993?

Craig Perham: I believe so, yes.

Bill Streever: I'd be curious to know more about the history of how those regulations came about. In other places where there are marine mammal issues, people are still, let's face it, ignoring the law entirely. And up here in Alaska, we've been following it more closely that anyone else. I was just wondering if you knew anything about the evolution of that in 1993, who applied for those regulations? I really don't know. I suspect it was probably BP, but I don't know that.

Craig Perham: I believe you're right. U.S. Fish and Wildlife was monitoring polar bears in at much lower level, and I believe probably a couple of instances elevated that to the point where it needed to be a little bit more structured. There was a polar bear that had actually been killed, in defense of life, in Camden Bay, I believe in 1991, and that may have triggered something. I believe it was BP that actually petitioned for the first set of incidental take regulations. I could be wrong, but if I remember right, I think it was BP.

Bill Streever: I guess I was getting more at what got people engaged in Alaska, whereas elsewhere in the country they are still ignoring the law?

Craig Perham: I see. All right.

Bill Streever: Was it that shooting of the polar bear, those ones that were poisoned? I don't know.

Craig Perham: It could have been. Maybe we can discuss this afterwards.

Michael Castellini: I have two questions. One, related to the question you just asked. But I'll ask the other one first. Maybe it's not a fair question to ask you, since you've come in from the management side. But even if polar bears weren't a management issue, they'd be interesting animals to study. When you were talking about the research that was going on, even the research from U.S. Geological Survey (USGS) you put with a management spin. I understand that, because you come from the management side. What I wanted to ask is, if you could spend a minute, that you could tell us what else USGS is doing perhaps that has something to do with the fact that they are interested in animals as opposed to it's a management problem.

Craig Perham: Sure. Let me see if I can put my researcher hat on rather than my manager hat. Actually both groups do work very closely together. But currently these are projects that USGS, which holds the research arm of polar bears: We have got a den-emergence study still going on which is looking at when do the bears emerge and what do they do when they emerge out there on the Slope. That's a joint project between both of our groups that has been going on since 2001. USGS is also gearing up to do their capture work, which is going to happen here in the springtime. They go from Barrow all the way to Kaktovik, spend six weeks up there, and capture as many bears as they can for population estimates. They feel this is one of the best population estimates going right now, in terms of polar bears. They have a Ph.D. student working on that. And there are some aspects in there of climate change as well. They've been doing, I'm going to call it by its initials, IFSAR. They've been looking at gathering polar bear, potential polar bear denning habitat by looking as satellite imagery. So they have been using that, fine-tuning and ground-truthing to see where polar-bear denning habitat is in NPRA. They've already got it between the Canning and the Colville rivers, based on aerial photos. And they did a little bit of work out on the Arctic last year. They just feed in the characteristics, slope, aspect, location, of all the dens, the known dens that they've gone out and measured. U.S. Fish and Wildlife is using a lot of their data right now, even though it's preliminary data, to tell... We use FLIR imagery, which is forward-looking infrared. It's a form of mitigation to look for polar bear dens. And the way that we fine-tune that is we use that as an indicator of where to fly and where to send the plane. So we don't fly the whole coastline, we just fly those pieces that are designated as potential denning habitat. They're in charge of the AMTAP program. I know there are other projects that they're doing or they have done recently. We've collaborated with them on an acoustic study. I never alluded to it but it was in the background there. We were looking at the attenuation of noise in artificial dens, basically recording vibration and sounds.

Tom Newbury: You showed a slide of the area within which the incidental take regulations would apply, and it excluded ANWR. Do the regulations actually mention ANWR, or is it just that no oil and gas activity is allowed in ANWR?

Craig Perham: That is a good question. That actually came from industry. In the petition that industry gives us, that we review, they set up the geographic location or the region that they want to have incidental take regulations in. And it has always excluded the ANWR.

Tom Newbury: Does that mean that, if Congress passes or changes the provisions about ANWR, that there would have to be some changes in the incidental take regulations?

Craig Perham: That sounds like a beer question! Yes. The short answer is yes. We've had discussions on that one actually.

Bill Streever: I think the important thing to understand is every time you want special regulations you have to petition. And we aren't going to petition in an area where we're not going. So if somebody wanted to do something like build a nuclear reactor on the Slope, they would have to petition as well. Right, Craig?

Craig Perham: Pretty much.

Tom Newbury: ... [not audible] .. petition to bait bears ?

Craig Perham: Let me see, ...baiting bears ... It's a conundrum, because right now the only industry, the only citizens, that have applied for incidental take anywhere in the State of Alaska is the oil and gas industry on the North Slope. They haven't even applied for it for, say, walrus or sea otters in Cook Inlet. And those operators up there feel that it is in their best interest to have this regulation or this program in place. But you are right. Anything that technically involves a take or potential incidental take should really have a set of regulations. But who's going to do that? You end up getting into, involved in all the tour operators down in Resurrection Bay and the like, as well. I don't know.

Jeff Childs: As you were running through your presentation, the information was largely anchored in the terrestrial environment, and yet polar bears are marine mammals. They utilize the offshore environment. I'm curious to know what recommendations came out of the workshop were for research and monitoring polar bears in the offshore environment?

Craig Perham: I think that goes in hand with some of the broader research recommendations. Nested within habitat alteration was the fact that the three most important habitats that the group decided on was the sea-ice habitat, the coastal habitat, and the denning habitat, which can be coastal, or sea ice. I think where the consensus of the group was, in terms of the importance of this offshore area, the marine environment, it came in the broader research recommendations for looking at and continuing to study, both through the population estimation of the southern Beaufort Sea stock, as well as looking at the Chukchi Sea. Those are important components of this offshore area, as important components of both of them. There's already a component in the Beaufort Sea, with the climate change. U.S. Fish and Wildlife conducts aerial surveys in the fall, to see where the bears are hanging out during that time. We've looked at that ice-edge component, where that ice edge is, in comparison with all these bears. And I expect that that will continue in the future, as these surveys continue. It is a very big, important part of it, and I believe it's incorporated into these much broader studies, population studies.

STATUS OF KING AND COMMON EIDERS MIGRATING
PAST POINT BARROW, ALASKA

Robert Suydam[1], Lori Quakenbush[2], Mike Knoche[3], and Rita Frantz[1]

[1]North Slope Borough Department of Wildlife Management, Barrow, AK, (907) 852-0350, Fax (907) 852-0351, E-mail: Robert.Suydam@north-slope.org; Rita.Frantz@north-slope.org
[2]Alaska Department of Fish and Game, 1300 College Rd., Fairbanks, AK, (907) 459-7214, Fax (907) 452-6410, E-mail: lori_quakenbush@fishgame.state.ak.us
[3]University of Alaska, Department of Biology and Wildlife, Fairbanks, AK, (907) 474-5505
E-mail: mikeknoche@hotmail.com

King (*Somateria spectabilis*) and Common (*S. mollissima v-nigra*) eiders migrate past Point Barrow, Alaska between wintering areas in and adjacent to the Bering Sea and nesting areas in northern Alaska and northwestern Canada. Based on standardized migration counts, both populations declined by more than 50% between 1953 and 1996. King Eiders declined from approximately 800,000 to 350,000 birds and Common Eiders declined from about 150,000 to 70,000 birds. Preliminary results from migration counts in summer/fall 2002, spring and summer/fall 2003, and spring 2004 indicate that the King Eider population has increased (summer/fall 2002 estimate = 486,625, 95%CI $\pm$ 85,862; spring 2003 estimate = 356,814; 95% CI $\pm$ 86,821; summer/fall 2003 estimate = 405,820, 95%CI $\pm$ 76,598; spring 2004 estimate = 592,889, 95%CI $\pm$ 171,127). Additionally, the Common Eider population also seems to have increased (spring 2003 estimate = 117,003; 95% CI $\pm$ 25,998; spring 2004 estimate = 109,449, 95%CI $\pm$ 32,835). Fall migration counts after early September provide an index of production for King Eiders because very few adults are seen migrating past Barrow after early September. In 2002, about 110,000 King Eiders migrated past Point Barrow after early September indicating that a moderate number of eiders were produced in 2002. In 2003, only about 30,000 birds migrated past Barrow after early September suggesting a year with low production. Obtaining an index of production for Common Eiders is difficult because many adults molt in the eastern Beaufort Sea. These adult Common Eiders migrate past Barrow in later September and October with young making it difficult to differentiate young birds from females in the large migrating flocks.

Discussion:

Susanne Miller: I was just wondering where they over-winter. Where are they coming up from, for both common and king eiders?

Robert Suydam: Actually, for three of the eider species, we had virtually or very little information on wintering locations which in the early 1990s really prompted a lot of satellite telemetry work. Margaret Petersen started with Spectacled eiders, and she figured out they are all wintering in the middle of the Bering Sea. We now have better information on King eiders and Common eiders, in particular linking nesting areas with wintering area. We have learned a great deal in the last five or ten years. Lynn Dixon has been collecting satellite telemetry data on King and Common eiders. Laura Phillips has also been focused on with King eiders. King eiders seem to winter along both sides of the Bering Sea and relatively near the shore.

Michael Castellini: What are your plans for the future now that you've established one good data point? And where do you go from here?

Robert Suydam: In the near term, we need to finish cleaning up the data, complete the analysis, finish the report for Coastal Marine Institute, and submit a paper for publication. I'm hesitant to say that I want to do more counts right away. They are a lot of work; there are a lot of different aspects to them. Also, I don't know that we really need to do counts again right away. Our counts in the mid 1990s and our recent counts more or less are all saying the same thing. All the confidence intervals are pretty close in terms of their overlapping. So I guess my recommendation is wait another five or ten years and do another two or three or four counts. I think that there are a lot of other recommendations for information that's needed for all of the eiders, since their biology is so poorly known. The declines that we think we saw in the mid 1990s are one of the things that has prompted Rebecca McGuire's on the breeding biology of King eider work, which she'll talk about momentarily. Is that a good segue?

Discussion from the Barrow IUM:

Dick Prentki: The timing of the decline for those ducks looks quite similar to when the regime changed in the Gulf of Alaska and Bering Sea. Do you think it could be related to that?

Robert Suydam: For all of the eider populations the numbers seemed to decline in the 1970s and 1980s. A lot of us have thought that it could be due to changes in the Bering Sea. Whatever the cause for those changes, who knows? A lot of us felt that the breeding areas are so remote and have had so little human influence, that it seemed likely that it was a winter phenomenon that was caused the populations to decline. That is one of the leading hypotheses on why the eider populations have declined.

POPULATION STRUCTURE OF COMMON EIDERS NESTING ON COASTAL BARRIER ISLANDS ADJACENT TO OIL FACILITIES IN THE BEAUFORT SEA

Sarah A. Sonsthagen[1], Kevin G. McCracken [1], Richard B. Lanctot[2], Sandra L. Talbot [3], and Kim T. Scribner[4]

[1]Institute of Arctic Biology, University of Alaska Fairbanks, Fairbanks, AK 99775
[2]U.S. Fish and Wildlife Service, Migratory Bird Management
1011 East Tudor Road, MS 201, Anchorage, AK 99503
[3] U.S. Geological Survey, Biological Resources Division, Alaska Science Center,
1011 East Tudor Road, MS 701, Anchorage, AK 99503
[4]Department of Fisheries and Wildlife, 13 Natural Resources Building,
Michigan State University, East Lansing, MI 48824

Common eider (*Somateria mollissima*) populations have exhibited declines throughout parts of their range including Alaska, western Canada, southern Hudson Bay, and eastern Finland. While the reason for this decline is unknown, factors such as, increased gull and arctic fox predation, development, or other anthropogenic effects may be playing a role in the decreasing eider populations. These birds nest primarily on barrier islands and coastal brackish waters. Data suggest that adult females and young exhibit a high degree of natal and nest site fidelity to islands, thus potentially creating genetically unique island groups relative to neighboring islands. In contrast, males exhibit high natal and breeding dispersal distances, which may have a homogenizing effect on eider population genetics.

We investigated population structure of Common eiders breeding in the Beaufort Sea and throughout their distribution using three types of molecular markers (microsatellite genotypes, mitochondrial [mtDNA] control region, and two nuclear intron sequences) that differ in their mode of inheritance and rate of mutation. Using markers that differ in their mode of inheritance and rate of evolution enables us to assess whether population structure is due to female or male breeding behavior and how long populations have diverged from each other.

We collected blood and feather samples from 309 female Common eiders breeding on two island groups in the Beaufort Sea: 5 islands in Simpson Lagoon and 7 islands in Mikkelsen Bay. Genotypic microsatellite data were collected at 14 loci and sequence data were collected for 545 bp mtDNA control region and two nuclear introns, *lamin* A and *gapdh*. We did not observe any significant pairwise F_{ST} values at the microsatellite loci or significant pairwise Φ_{ST} values at nuclear intron *gapdh*. However, we did detect significant pairwise comparisons between one island in Mikkelsen Bay (Duchess Is.) and all islands located in Simpson Lagoon within mtDNA, with Φ_{ST} values ranging from 0.135 − 0.271. Additionally, we observed significant pairwise comparisons within nuclear intron *lamin* A between and among islands in Mikkelsen Bay and Simpson Lagoon with pairwise Φ_{ST} values ranging from 0.025 – 0.205.

We also collected microsatellite genotypes, mtDNA and nuclear intron sequences from 20 populations representing 5 subspecies: *S. m. v-nigra*; Aleutain Is. (n = 48), Yukon-Kuskokwim Delta (4 sites; n = 124 birds), Beaufort Sea (2 sites; n = 196), and Kent Peninsula (n = 41), *S. m. borealis*; Baffin Island (n = 15), Hudson Straits (n = 28), Southampton Island (n = 52), and Mansel Island (n = 3), *S. m. sendentaria*; Belcher Islands (n = 20), *S. m. dresseri*; New Brunswick (n = 40), and Nova Scotia (n = 40), and *S. m. mollissima*; Svalbard (n = 37), Tromsø (n = 38) , Soderskar (n = 27), and Russia (n = 12). Within mtDNA, there were high levels of population structuring with Φ_{ST} values ranging from 0.096 – 0.703. There were two haplotype groups present with one haplotype group predominately represented by individuals breeding in the Beaufort Sea and the other group represented by individuals breeding in Aleutians, Yukon-Kuskokwim Delta, Canada, and Scandinavia. Within the nuclear markers, we observed similar patterns across the microsatellite and nuclear intron data. In general, there were few significant pairwise comparisons within subspecies and little to moderate structure among subspecies. For both introns, there were two allele groups present which likely correspond to the two haplotype groups we observed in mtDNA.

Based on mtDNA analyses, Common eiders breeding in the Mikkelsen Bay are genetically distinct from eiders breeding in Simpson Lagoon. Since there are no significant pairwise comparisons within island groups, female eiders breeding in the Beaufort Sea are likely philopatric to island groups rather than individual islands. This differs from what has been shown for other eider populations where they have been reported to be philopatric to specific islands.

The existence of 2 allele and haplotype groups suggest that Common eiders were historically subdivided in two separate refugium during the last glaciation. Birds breeding on the Beaufort Sea were likely colonized by a refugium separate to the other studied populations. Where as birds breeding in the Aleutians and Yukon-Kuskokwim Delta appear to be more genetically related to Canadian and Scandinavian populations. This is based on the cline in mtDNA haplotype frequencies, which indicates a stepwise postglacial colonization of Scandinavia, Canada, Yukon-Kuskokwim Delta and Aleutian Islands in a ring distribution. Shared alleles and haplotypes between localities suggest that recent gene flow via female and, to a higher degree, male dispersal has occurred. Male mediated gene flow has likely had a homogenizing effect on the population structure, as there is little to no genetic differentiation among populations that share wintering grounds i.e., within subspecies. Differences in the levels of genetic population subdivision between maternally and bi-parentally inherited markers indicates that female common eiders are exhibiting a high degree of philopatry where as males are the dispersing agents.

Discussion:

Charles Monnett: That's a great example of a Coastal Marine Institute (CMI) study that's really working the way it ought to. They used a small amount of CMI money and huge amount of leverage to expand way beyond the original scope of work. Because when they first started, all they were going to look at were those few islands out there. And you can see they went all over the world with this. You're to be congratulated for that.

Sarah Sonsthagen: Thank you.

Sandy Talbot: Did you assess the relationship among individuals within your islands to avoid over sampling family groups?

Sarah Sonsthagen: Yes. Because we had so many microsatellite loci, we were able to get a probability of identity. I'm not sure what it was, but it was in the billions. It was much larger than what the actual eider population is on the Beaufort. So if we had identical genotypes across all loci for two samples, it was mainly between feather and blood samples. We removed the feather samples from our analysis, because it's a good chance that they were the same bird.

Rick Lanctot: I had one question as well. Basically you are saying that the North Slope population is genetically distinct? Would you then go so far as to say that that should be managed as a separate population, especially in light of the fact that the productivity on a lot of those islands isn't doing so well? Where would you go with that in terms of recommendations?

Sarah Sonsthagen: I've never had a management class in my life; take that into consideration when I answer this. But I think there's something special going on there. And from what I understand, it's important to preserve genetic integrity, especially if something might potentially happen to these birds, if they are really declining. I think that they should be considered special, if anything, and looked at as a group, rather that just grouping all of the Alaskan eiders together. I would say let's look at the North Slope eiders together, the Y-K Delta birds, and then the Aleutians birds are also showing high levels of structuring. So I think, because they are exhibiting such high degrees of natal and breeding site fidelity within the females, that we need to of address that and look at them as such.

Rick Lanctot: Another thing I would like you to comment on. You used 14 different microsets? And how many are typically used for a study like this?

Sarah Sonsthagen: It depends on the species, but I think you can generally get away with eight. We were going a little bit more than what you typically see published recently. You see about eight to ten, I think. We just thought, with the big scheme of things, we might as well do a couple more.

Rick Lanctot: So are you more likely to see differences using more microsets or fewer microsets?

Sarah Sonsthagen: I tried to pick loci that had a range in the number of alleles. Ones that had few alleles that would likely pick up more historic structuring and those that had higher number of alleles that would maybe tease out more of the inter-island differences. There's always that debate, if you are getting too much variability in the data that you are muddying up your results. With our study now, I don't think that is the case, because I didn't have a large number of alleles. I think a couple of loci had around 25. In other papers they suggest that when you have 50-100 alleles you can start to see problems with variability masking structure. I think we have a good number and range of alleles at our microsatellite loci and I think the main reason why we are not seeing structure at the microsatellite loci is because males are moving around quite a bit.

Unidentified: Common eiders are kind of special in that they do have recognized subspecies. But your various samples of *v-nigra* clustered separately from each other, so would you say *v-nigra* is an artificial construct?

Sarah Sonsthagen: Could you repeat it again?

Unidentified: You had multiple samples of *v-nigra*, like North Slope and western Alaska. But your western Alaska birds grouped in your analyses with Canadian and Scandinavian birds, rather than with other *v-nigra*. So do you doubt the integrity of *v-nigra* as a valid subspecies?

Sarah Sonsthagen: I think it is. If you even just look at just microsatellite and then *gapdh*, they are grouping out within themselves with that principal component analysis. You saw them way on the other side and grouping very tightly together. And also with *gapdh*, they pretty much all shared the same haplotype, or alleles. So I think it is valid subspecies.

BREEDING BIOLOGY AND HABITAT USE OF KING EIDERS ON THE COASTAL PLAIN OF NORTHERN ALASKA

Rebecca McGuire[1], Abby Powell[1] and Robert Suydam[2]

[1]Alaska Cooperative Fish and Wildlife Research Unit, University of Alaska, Fairbanks
(907) 474-5505, Email: ftrlm@uaf.edu, ffanp@uaf.edu
[2]Department of Wildlife Management, North Slope Borough, Barrow, AK 99723
(907) 852-0350, Email: Robert.Suydam@north-slope.org

Little is known about the breeding biology of King eiders (*Somateria spectabilis*), partly because they typically nest in remote areas in low densities. The western North American population of King eiders declined by more than 50% between 1976 and 1996 for unknown reasons (Suydam et al. 2000). Additionally, NPR-A is being leased for oil and gas exploration and may potentially be developed. Within the northeast planning area of NPR-A is the highest known density of nesting King eiders on the north slope of Alaska (Larned et al. 2003). During the summers of 2002, 2003, and 2004 we studied King Eiders in an area to the southeast of Teshekpuk Lake, and in the Kuparuk oilfields on the North Slope of Alaska to evaluate the potential impacts of development and to provide information on their basic breeding biology and habitat use.

We found between 31 and 44 King eider nests at each site in each year; most nests were near water, often on peninsulas or on islands in wetland basins. Apparent nest success ranged between 17.5% and 42.9% and is not significantly different between the sites. Nest success is slightly higher on islands on average (B_{island}= 0.66, 95% CL = 0.26, 1.06). Clutch size averaged 4.2 eggs/nest with no differences between sites or among years. Females had lower incubation constancy at Teshekpuk (95%) than at Kuparuk (99%). Females nesting on the mainland took more recesses each day (1.05 day^{-1} ± 0.166, n= 21) than those nesting on islands (0.70 day^{-1} ± 0.139, n= 22). Mean recess length was between 18.4 and 53.0 minutes and average recess start times varied between 2:26PM and 3:32PM.

Nest success is quite low in King eider, with nests being vulnerable to a number of different avian and mammalian predators. Incubation behavior has not been previously investigated in King eider. Incubating birds face conflicting selection pressures; maintaining a favorable thermal environment for embryo development, maintaining a favorable energy balance for themselves, and minimizing the risk of predation on themselves and their eggs. King eider are near the extremes of the waterfowl continuum in severity of climate and reliance on nutrient reserves so are an interesting species in which to study the incubation behavior. We found incubation constancy to be very high with females consistently taking more and longer breaks at Teshekpuk than they do at Kuparuk, resulting in lower incubation constancy. This pattern was consistent during the three years of the study. The Teshekpuk study site is further inland and the habitat is somewhat different; wetland basins tend to be smaller and there are more dry uplands separating the wetlands. However, nest density is higher at Teshekpuk within wetland systems (pers. obs.) and the site is within the highest density of breeding pairs of King Eider on the North Slope of Alaska (Larned et al 2003).

Literature Cited:

Larned, W., R. Stehn, and R. Platte. 2003. Eider breeding population survey arctic coastal plain, Alaska 2003. U.S. Fish and Wildlife Service.

Suydam, R.S., D.L. Dickson, J.B. Fadely, and L.T. Quakenbush. 2000. Population declines of King and Common Eiders of the Beaufort Sea. Condor. 102: 219-222.

Discussion:

Bill Streever: You had a plot up there that showed nest temperature, after the female left the nest. It seemed like one of the lines decreased then increased. Was that because the daytime temperature got warmer? What made it go back up before mom got home?

Rebecca McGuire: There are some very slight increases on some of them. That's probably because the sun came out from behind the cloud and hit it, or something like that. But I really looked at the first few temperature records, when it's really dropping steeply.

PROTOCOL TO DEFLECT MIGRATING BOWHEAD WHALES AWAY FROM AN OIL SPILL: STATUS REPORT

W. John Richardson, Ph.D.

LGL Ltd., environmental research associates
22 Fisher St., POB 280, King City, Ont. L7B 1A6, Canada
(905) 833-1244, Fax (905) 833-1255, E-mail wjr@lgl.com

Bowhead whales avoid various types of human activities, often based on receiving sounds from those activities. Bowheads may also react to killer whales or to their sounds. The purpose of this ongoing project is to develop protocols for keeping bowhead whales away from any large oil spill that might occur off the North Slope of Alaska. Although a major oil spill is assumed to be very unlikely, MMS considered it prudent to initiate development of a contingency plan to reduce the potential effects of a major oil spill by taking advantage of the tendency of bowheads to avoid certain activities and stimuli. The approach includes the following steps: analyze literature on potential methods (e.g., noise) for excluding or deflecting cetaceans; consult with North Slope residents regarding how they might participate in planning and (if necessary) implementing a deflection effort; develop a coordinated field protocol that would use the best available methods to keep bowheads away from a hypothetical oil spill over days and/or weeks; and provide recommendations for improving methods for deflecting bowheads. Although the project title refers to migrating bowheads, bowheads engaged in feeding and other activities are being considered. The project team includes Applied Sociocultural Research, Barrow Arctic Sciences Consortium, Greeneridge Sciences Inc., and the North Slope Borough Department of Wildlife Management in addition to prime contractor LGL Ltd. and project sponsor MMS Alaska OCS Region.

The Literature Search and Analysis has involved reviewing responses of bowheads (and, in less detail, other baleen whales) to boats, aircraft, air guns, projected non-biological sounds, projected killer whale calls, and offshore development activities, along with oil and chemical dispersants. Permitting issues are being considered. In parallel with the above, initial community meetings were arranged in Barrow, Nuiqsut and Kaktovik to discuss the project concept, possible deterrent approaches, and potential local involvement. Those meetings, and initial contacts with oil industry and Alaska Clean Seas representatives, occurred in February–March 2005. Further discussions with North Slope communities and industry are anticipated.

Based on those initial tasks, proposed deterrent approaches will be developed. It will be necessary to plan for different approaches depending on season, physical situation, bowhead activities at the time and place of the spill (e.g., migrating vs. feeding), and available logistics. A preliminary list of possible approaches has been identified, and their likely practicality and effectiveness in different situations are being evaluated. Based on an initial assessment, some of the more promising approaches (if necessary equipment is available and deployable in the circumstances) could include boats, helicopters, airguns, playbacks of killer whale sounds, and perhaps use of some other acoustic sources. When the draft deterrence protocol is completed, it will be made available to stakeholders for review and discussion. Additional community discussions are planned on the North Slope at this stage, prior to completion of a final report taking account of all comments.

In developing recommended protocols, the project team recognizes inherent limitations in the concept. Bowhead reactions to various stimuli are variable, and not all individuals show avoidance. Also, there are likely to be severe logistical and environmental constraints that—despite any amount of advance planning, training, permitting, and equipment stockpiling—may limit or prevent implementation. The potentially intense activity associated with an oil containment and cleanup effort may account for much of the deterrent effect that might ultimately be achieved, and that needs to be built into the protocol.

Discussion:

Robert Suydam: I would like to thank MMS for being responsive to people on the North Slope. It is my understanding that this project really started because someone from the North Slope Borough planning department made a suggestion, at a mutual aid drill, that if there was an oil spill in the ocean that we should go out and try to keep bowheads from swimming through it. So I would like to thank MMS for pursuing this project, in particular, because of that.

At the Alaska Eskimo Whaling Commission (AEWC) meeting, when this project was presented, there was very strong concern about the approach of the project. The community meetings were held, as you mentioned in Phase III, which was after the literature review and analysis and evaluation of the different techniques. The AEWC strongly felt left out of the loop; that they should have been part of the evaluation process not just a part afterward. So there is definitely much concern about that. It seems that if this project is to go forward and the permitting is going to be approved, the AEWC and whaling captains in the various villages will need to be on board with this project in order for it to be successful and effective.

So I guess my questions are: How will LGL deal with public comments heard at the meetings? I know you said that you would address them. But certainly people in the past have been very concerned when they go to public meetings and make comments about things, that they feel like their statements aren't really addressed or taken into account? So how will your study team deal with the comments that have been made? Secondly, will you go back and start over and revisit the literature review with AEWC and the whaling captains' input?

John Richardson: The literature review was not completed at the time of those meetings and we have not yet begun to prepare the draft protocols. In fact, the purpose of convening the community meetings was to do some of the things that you just mentioned were needed. Likewise, going back to the North Slope later to follow up on suggestions. The intent was to hold those community meetings at as early stage as possible in the project. The earliest that could have happened was in November 2004 after the fall whaling season. It would not have been practical to hold the meetings during the whaling season. We tried to arrange meeting dates in late fall, but could not find acceptable meeting dates then. The meetings were in fact held in early February 2005, as early in the project as they could be arranged. The draft protocols have not yet been prepared, so the discussion at those meetings can and will be taken into account in formulating the protocols. Also, we do plan to go back to the North Slope to follow up on the suggestions, and to discuss how they have been used in formulating the proposed protocol, prior to finalizing our recommendations.

One other comment: I was not at the community meetings, but other people from our group were there. Although I do not know the exact wording of some of the comments that were made, my understanding is that many of the comments pertained primarily to the general concerns about prospects for increasing offshore oil development in the Beaufort Sea. Those concerns are somewhat peripheral to this specific project and its objectives.

Robert Suydam: The people on the North Slope are concerned about offshore exploration and development. In this particular project, though, there was great concern about the lack of consultation before the meeting. My guess is that if you have a follow up meeting and show up with a finalized or draft final report that is not going to alleviate concerns. I think the AEWC wants to have an influence in the development of that report and development of the analyses. If there is any way at all that you can go back and meet with individual captains or the AEWC to help with the analysis and evaluation of the techniques, I think that would be very beneficial.

John Richardson: I appreciate your comments. Certainly, when we do go back, it was always intended that we would come with suggestions, a draft protocol, by no means a final document. I understand that you are saying that there is an interest in arranging additional consultation at an earlier stage than that.

Richard Newman: Do we have some allies in this process of keeping bowheads away from oil, that is the bowheads themselves? They are quite intelligent creatures. Do we have any information on that?

John Richardson: In the sense of whether they would react to the oil itself? Specifically for bowheads, we do not know much about that. However, there is some information for certain other species of marine mammals, including some other baleen whales, indicating that they do not always avoid spilled oil and will occasionally swim into it. There may be other people in the room who know more about that than I do.

Brad Smith: Regarding some of the concerns that Robert Suydam had mentioned, one thing that we are looking for is that the protocols that are developed through your study would then be taken and, in the spirit of the agreements for cooperative management of bowheads with the AEWC, we would try to implement those protocols through a series of discussions and meetings, not only with AEWC but with the various whaling captain associations. One of the concerns that I got during the convention, and it is similar to what we see over the use of dispersants, was that there was fear in the community that these hazing protocols would leap-frog the mechanical efforts to remove the spill or things that would otherwise be done to respond to the spill. I think that is a reasonable concern. One of the suggestions that I would offer is that at some point we develop a decision tree or some sort of dichotomous decision tree that we could develop along with the natives that would clearly point out that mechanical removal and all of the other efforts would precede or at least be considered in the context of responding to bowhead whales and intentional hazing. I think that is something that would be important whether it is developed through your study or through the efforts to implement the protocols.

John Richardson: Thank you.

Bill Streever: I would like to partly reiterate what Robert Suydam said. Sometimes when these things are taken up to the villages and are handled the way they were, reflects badly on others who weren't even present or consulted. It is kind of frustrating for us. We would encourage you to do the same thing and also to pre-consult with BP and anyone else who might have "good neighbor" policies in place, etc.

But I actually did have a question as well. I was wondering what are people doing elsewhere in the world where the likelihood of spills is probably higher like in the Gulf of Mexico where there are also whales? Are there hazing practices in place in the Gulf of Mexico for whales or in California with seals and sea lions?

John Richardson: There are many hazing programs for other types of marine mammals in different parts of the world. Most of these programs or plans are for other purposes, including efforts to keep marine mammals away from aquaculture facilities. There probably are some other plans in place for oil spill contingency purposes but I do not know much about the latter. If there are people present who are aware of those and know about the details, I would be interested in talking with them. As to how things were handled before and during the community meetings, we have a somewhat different perspective on this than has been mentioned in the previous comments. However, whatever the history, we want to move this project forward in a way that is productive and agreeable to all.

Mark Major: I just wanted to applaud LGL and the MMS for incorporating the oil industry and Alaska Clean Seas (ACS) into this whole project. That seemed to be missing when the Barrow meetings were held. I think that is the right answer. I don't know at what levels or what we can do, but certainly it is worth talking about and see what the oil industry and ACS could do. Part of ACS's mission is to protect wildlife resources. So I am sure there is something that can be done.

John Richardson: From the start of the project, it was planned that there would be consultation with ACS in parallel with the community meetings. That consultation in fact did not begin until after those meetings, but is now underway. Also, it has always been planned that industry would be invited to provide comments on the proposed deflection protocols.

ANALYSIS OF COVARIANCE OF HUMAN ACTIVITIES AND SEA ICE IN RELATION TO FALL MIGRATIONS OF BOWHEAD WHALES

W. John Richardson, Ph.D.[1]
Senior author of report: Bryan F.J. Manly, Ph.D.[2]

[1] LGL Ltd., environmental research associates
22 Fisher St., POB 280, King City, Ont. L7B 1A6, Canada
(905) 833-1244, Fax (905) 833-1255, E-mail wjr@lgl.com
[2] Western EcoSystems Technology Inc., Cheyenne, WY
(307) 634-1756; bmanly@west-inc.com

This study aimed to develop an analysis approach for investigating whether and how the distribution of bowhead whales in the Alaskan Beaufort Sea during autumn is affected by human activities, while simultaneously investigating and allowing for influences of ice and other natural environmental factors on bowhead distribution and sightability. The study was based on analysis of aerial survey, industrial activity, and environmental data collected during the 1996, 1997 and 1998 autumn migration seasons.

This project was one of a series of related MMS-sponsored projects. The first of these retrospectively compiled a "Human Activities Database" (HAD) documenting oil industry and other activities in the Alaskan Beaufort Sea during 1979 to 1999 (P. Wainwright, 2002, OCS Study MMS 02-0071). One component of that study assessed the feasibility of using data from the HAD plus already-available aerial survey data on bowheads in the Alaskan Beaufort Sea to assess influences of human activities, ice, and other environmental factors on bowhead distribution and sighting probability. The present project was intended as an initial implementation of the recommended multivariate approach to a subset of the available data, from one or a few years. It was recognized from the outset that, to address the many questions and hypotheses about factors influencing bowhead distribution and sighting probability, further analysis incorporating data from additional years would be needed.

The data from 1996-98 used here came from MMS-BWASP aerial surveys and from site-specific aerial surveys sponsored by BP and Western Geophysical around their seismic vessels. There was no offshore drilling during autumn in those years, and all 3 years were light-ice years. A Poisson regression approach was developed and applied to quantify the number of bowhead sightings in small (5 x 5 km) areas along the flight lines in relation to human activity variables, natural and environmental variables, and factors that might affect bowhead sightability. The analysis showed that, for 1996-98, natural and environmental factors that were significantly related to bowhead sighting probability included distance from shore, water depth, longitude, survey type (BWASP vs. industry), and visibility. After allowing for those factors, number of sightings was shown to be reduced near active seismic vessels, consistent with results of previous analyses of the same data, but now accounting for the simultaneous influences of covariates.

This analysis of 3 years' data, completed in March 2004, developed a procedure for applying a multivariate approach to combined BWASP and site-specific aerial survey data concerning bowheads in the Alaskan Beaufort Sea. A multivariate approach allows us to simultaneously address several hypotheses about combined effects of human-activity, environmental, and sightability variables on bowhead sighting probability. With further work, model fit could be improved to better characterize the spatial and temporal scale of effects, and degree of avoidance. Adding data from other years with different human activities (e.g., drill ships) and environmental conditions (e.g., more ice) would allow the generality of model to be improved. However, for some years in the early 1990s, missing data for certain human activities and sightability factors is a complication. For years prior to 1990, those ancillary data are probably too incomplete for use in a multivariate analysis of corresponding aerial survey data. Updating the HAD beyond 1999 would be necessary before more recent BWASP aerial survey results could be used.

Discussion:

Robert Suydam: I have a question on your comment about missing data. What data are missing, in terms of human activities? And what is the likelihood that those data gaps could be filled?

John Richardson: Some of the information about the survey conditions (sea state, visibility, and so on) during site-specific aerial surveys in the early 1990s has not been found, despite a considerable amount of effort trying to find those data in various archives. As to the missing information about certain industrial activities, I do not remember exactly which data are missing for which years. However, one example is that we have not been able to find detailed records of the icebreaker activities that occurred in support of the drill ship operations in the early 1990s in the Camden Bay area. There is some general information about ice breaking in those years but we have not found records of the specific times and locations of icebreaking activities. Among others, Mark Major has expended quite a bit of effort trying to find relevant data from the early 1990s in the archives available to him, but with no success.

Cleve Cowles: I noticed that during the previous talk we really have a great representation of the parties that have been interested in this topic over the years from NMFS, industry, MMS, local governments, etc. I would like to say that John mentioned in his report the Human Activities Database. In your packet there is a list of completed OCS study Reports. The report number for that project is MMS 2002-0071 (Wainwright 2002). For those of you who have been following these matters since the late 1970s, like me, I recommend it. It is small report but with some very useful information. I recommend that you pick it up and take a look at it. You can access it through MMS' website or call me if you can't get it that way.

Bill Streever: One of your earlier slides with or without seismic boat activity, it was interesting to me because with the seismic boat the highest concentration band was lost. It wasn't just deflected out. The light blue band narrowed and the yellow band disappeared from that part of the chart. Did the whales disperse or spent more time underwater? Do you have any thoughts on what was driving that?

John Richardson: We know quite a lot about what the whales did during the 1996-1998 seismic programs from the site-specific monitoring studies that were done in those years (Miller et al. 1999; Richardson et al. 1999). But I don't think we should pay much attention to the detailed shape of the "gap" in the distribution evident on the map "predicted" by the fitted statistical model. The model has not been refined to the point that it can depict those details accurately. It is at a preliminary stage at this point. We do know that the bowheads were deflected offshore as they passed the seismic vessel operating along or near the southern edge of the migration corridor in 1996-1998. We do not know how far to the east or to the west that effect extended., and I would not want to over-interpret what is shown on the maps generated from the present :"first-approximation" model.

Literature Cited:

Miller, G.W., R.E. Elliott, W.R. Koski, V.D. Moulton, and W.J. Richardson. 1999. Whales. Pages 5-1 to 5-109 *in* W.J. Richardson (ed.), Marine mammal and acoustical monitoring of Western Geophysical's open-water seismic program in the Alaska Beaufort Sea, 19989. LGL Rep. TA2230-3. Rep. from LGL Ltd., King City, Ont., and Greeneridge Sciences, Inc., Santa Barbara, CA for Western Geophysical, Houston, TX and U.S. National Marine Fisheries Service, Anchorage, AK, and Silver Spring, MD. 390 p.

Richardson, W.J., G.W. Miller, and C.R. Greene, Jr. 1999. Displacement of migrating bowhead whales by sounds from seismic surveys in shallow waters of the Beaufort Sea. J. Acoust. Soc. Am. 106(4, Pt.2): 2281.

Wainwright, P. 2002. GIS geospatial database of oil-industry and other human activity (1979-1999) in the Alaskan Beaufort Sea/ Public Report. OCS Study MMS 02-0071. Rep. from LGL Ltd., Sidney, B.C. for U.S. Minerals Management Service, Anchorage, AK. 91.p.

DISTRIBUTION AND ABUNDANCE OF HARBOR SEALS IN COOK INLET: SEASONAL VARIABILITY IN RELATION TO KEY LIFE HISTORY EVENTS

Peter L. Boveng[1], John L. Bengtson[1], and Michael A. Simpkins[2]

[1]National Marine Mammal Laboratory, Alaska Fisheries Science Center
NOAA Fisheries, 7600 Sand Point Way NE, Seattle, WA 98115
(206) 526-4244, E-mail: peter.boveng@noaa.gov
[2]Present address: Marine Mammal Commission, 4340 East-West Highway,
Suite 905, Bethesda, MD 20814, (301) 504-0087, E-mail: msimpkins@mmc.gov

Harbor seal populations have declined in several regions of Alaska during recent decades. Because harbor seals are key upper-trophic predators in the marine ecosystem, as well as an important subsistence resource for Alaska Natives, it is critical to assess accurately their abundance, distribution, and risk from human activities. The primary aim of this study is to quantify seasonal changes in the abundance and distribution of harbor seals at their haul-out sites in Cook Inlet, an area potentially at risk from oil spills and other industrial accidents.

Aerial surveys of harbor seal haul-out sites in Cook Inlet are the basis for estimates of abundance and distribution ashore during June and August, important periods for breeding and molting, and during October and April, when foraging and haul-out behavior are not constrained by those major life history events. During each of these months, the entire coastline of Cook Inlet is searched for haul-out sites and then all the known sites are surveyed daily for a period of 6-8 days during a series of diurnal low tides. Each daily flight takes place from 2 hours before, to 2 hours after the low tide. The survey observers, at an average altitude of 700 feet, count all harbor seals at small sites (≤10 seals) and photograph the larger sites for later counting in the laboratory.

Our series of surveys from June 2003 – June 2004 provided a preliminary view of the full seasonal pattern in abundance of harbor seals ashore. Numbers of seals counted in June of 2003 and 2004 were relatively high, exceeded only by the count in August 2003. These seasonal peaks in seal counts reflect the large amount of time seals spend ashore during the pupping period, in June, and the molting period, in July through mid-September. The counts were dramatically lower but more evenly distributed in October and April. This view of the year-round pattern in numbers of seals ashore will later be extended through 2005 and refined by adjustments for the conditions encountered during each survey, including date, time of day, tide height, and weather variables, all of which are known to affect the proportion of seals that haul out.

Time-lapse digital cameras were installed at selected haul-out sites to provide series of images (i.e., counts of seals) that will be used to develop and refine statistical models of the factors that influence the numbers of seals ashore. Finally, a companion study using satellite telemetry will provide data on movements, marine habitat use, and corrections to abundance estimates for seals missed because they were at sea during aerial surveys.

Discussion:

Brad Smith: Did you find any common attributes to the habitats that seemed to be important for pupping and molting during June and August?

Peter Boveng: Do you mean in terms of the substrates?

Brad Smith: That and proximity to salmon streams, anything that you might just broadly characterize as more important sites or is it just simply where they happen to be found?

Peter Boveng: We expect that some of those things will be apparent. We are not that far along in analyzing and bringing it in to a GIS-type analysis with the fisheries and other related data that we think would be helpful in explaining that variation. For now it is just sort of an observation that there is variation that needs to be explained.

SEASONAL DISTRIBUTION AND ABUNDANCE OF STELLER'S EIDERS IN COOK INLET, ALASKA

William W. Larned

U. S. Fish and Wildlife Service
1011 E. Tudor Road, Anchorage, AK 99503
(907) 260-0124, E-mail: William_Larned@fws.gov

Steller's eiders, listed as threatened under the Endangered Species Act, are known to winter in Cook Inlet, but distribution patterns are not well documented. The present study was designed to describe Steller's eider numbers and distribution during the winter months in Cook Inlet. We conducted aerial surveys of both east and west coastal areas from the shoreline to the 20-meter isobath, monthly from early December through early April. Steller's eiders and many other waterfowl are highly clustered during the winter in relation to food resources, a distribution that does not lend itself well to simple random or systematic sampling. Therefore, we used a combination approach, including both a systematic 30 percent sample grid of straight transects oriented perpendicular to the shoreline within the 20-m isobath limit, and a census of eider flocks containing 20 birds or more in the entire sampled area including interstices. Geographic coordinates of all observations were recorded using a laptop/GPS data recording system. To enhance detection as well as safety, we limited our surveys to relatively benign weather and sea conditions. Since neither complete coverage nor a detection rate study were feasible within our budget, we attempted to determine our ability to duplicate results by comparing observations using two survey aircraft spaced at least 30 minutes apart on the transects. This practice also enhanced safety of the single-engine, over-water aircraft operation.

Although the study was intended to cover two entire winters, we did not begin surveys until January 2004, due to delays in funding approval. Results from January through April of 2004 suggested a fairly consistent distribution of 900 to 1500 eiders in mid-winter on the east side of Cook Inlet, primarily near shore clustered in a few locations between Anchor Point and Clam Gulch, with lesser numbers and smaller flocks occupying offshore shoals between Anchor Point and the Homer spit. There were far fewer eiders during March and April, but distribution was similar. On the west side of Cook Inlet, most Steller's eiders were observed among shoals near the mouth of the Douglas River, while smaller numbers were recorded west of that in the Bruin Bay area. We found none north of Iniskin Bay. The highest total monthly estimate for the west side of the Inlet was 2067 on 15 March. Beginning in mid-February 2004, observations of sea otters were also recorded within the 600-meter sample strips, and observed densities were extrapolated within the search areas. Average estimates for sea otters, unadjusted for detection bias, were 276 for eastern, and 2,596 for western Cook Inlet. Nearly all observations were within Kachemak Bay on the east side, and south of Oil Bay on the west side.

Surveys have been completed for December 2004, and January and February 2005. Preliminary analysis indicates fewer eiders on the east side compared to the winter of 2003-2004. So far, on the west side of Cook Inlet, distribution and abundance of Steller's eiders are more variable than those of the winter of 2003-2004. We have seen very few eiders in the Douglas River shoals area, where the majority were concentrated last year.

No discussion.

MOVEMENTS AND HABITAT USE OF HARBOR SEALS IN COOK INLET

Peter L. Boveng[1], John L. Bengtson[1], and Michael A. Simpkins[2]

[1]National Marine Mammal Laboratory, Alaska Fisheries Science Center,
NOAA Fisheries, 7600 Sand Point Way NE, Seattle, WA 98115,
(206) 526-4244, E-mail: peter.boveng@noaa.gov
[2]Present address: Marine Mammal Commission, 4340 East-West Highway,
Suite 905, Bethesda, MD 20814, (301) 504-0087, E-mail: msimpkins@mmc.gov

Harbor seals' use of haul-out sites ashore can be assessed by aerial survey counts, but because the seals are inconspicuous in the water, their movements and habitat use at sea can only be assessed by a tracking method such as satellite telemetry. We are studying the movements and marine habitat use of harbor seals in Cook Inlet by tracking individual seals and recording their diving behavior through the Argos geo-location and telemetry system.

Thirty-four harbor seals were captured and released in Cook Inlet between August 27 and September 1, 2004 at a variety of sites widely distributed around central Cook Inlet, including Aurora Rock, Bradley River, Iniskin Bay, Chinitna Bay (Gull Island), and Tuxedni Bay. Sex and age distributions were well represented in the sample of 17 males and 17 females; of the thirty-four seals captured, twenty-four were considered adults, nine were sub-adults, and one was a pup. Nineteen of the 34 seals captured (6 adult males, 5 adult females, 1 sub-adult male, 6 sub-adult females, 1 female pup) were fitted with Wildlife Computers® satellite-linked depth recorders (SDR). These recorders collect and transmit information on each seal's location, haul-out time, and diving behavior for assessments of seal movements and habitat use.

Between September 2004, and January 2005, some seals of all three age classes made forays into Shelikof Strait and the Gulf of Alaska around the Kodiak Archipelago. Other individuals, however, remained in close proximity to their tagging sites throughout the period. These initial observations highlight the large variation among individual seals' foraging strategies and habitat use. Population-level inference about movements and habitat use will require additional satellite telemetry records, anticipated from deployments of more SDRs in May and September 2005 and 2006.

The SDRs logged and transmitted records of each seal's time spent ashore and at sea, allowing detailed estimates of the proportion of seals missed because they were in the water during the aerial surveys in our companion study of harbor seal abundance. Combining the seasonal survey counts with corresponding estimates of haul-out proportion will provide a new opportunity to create multiple independent estimates of the total population size. The variability among these estimates will help to evaluate assumptions that have previously been necessary to convert Alaska-wide survey counts from August, the seals' molt period, into estimates of total abundance.

Discussion:

Michael Castellini: Kathy Frost did work in Prince William Sound after the oil spill with satellite tags. Some of her animals make these look like "world travelers." They stayed on the same rock. If I remember correctly, did she see a male/female difference in the animals' behavior? Do you have enough data? You've only done 19, so you may not have enough data yet. Is there even a hint that you might have a male/female difference in movement?

Peter Boveng: I haven't been bold enough to look at that with the sample size that we have. I expect that there will be from just what we know of harbor seals elsewhere. We are waiting to get a few more instruments out before looking at that level of detail.

Cleve Cowles: I was thinking about those seals in Inner Kachemak Bay and that they seem to be hanging out in one area and in the presentation from the yesterday that shows how plastic the behavior of marine mammals can be in relation to human activity. I even thought further in these last few minutes about how regulatory systems sometimes come up with a sense that there is a particular human activity that has really profound exposure considerations to marine mammals. Yet, what I see is an opportunity for some other agency, not necessarily MMS because we focus on the Outer Continental Shelf, to study that group of seals in inner Kachemak Bay. It could be that those are animals that are demonstrating habituation to human activities. Perhaps some fine scale radio tagging rather using satellites would help understand that. You mentioned that Kasitna Bay Research Reserve is interested in this. It might be something that the National Marine Fisheries Service might want to suggest that they follow up on. When I go down to Homer, I always see seals hanging around the boat harbor. I am curious if there is something that we can learn about the behavior of that group of seals that would tell us more about animal behavior and habituation. That might be something to think about for the future.

Peter Boveng: Thanks for that comment. Harbor seals do habituate in some cases. There are some examples from Kachemak Bay. One of the sites that we routinely survey is a floating structure in Halibut Cove lagoon. Seals have hauled out there in great numbers with boats all around. It is obviously some man-made structure to begin with. Just in general, at some of those sites in Kachemak Bay, because of all the small vessel traffic, the seals are somewhat habituated to certain human activities. A nice extension on the study, at some point, would be to learn a little bit more about that on a fine scale.

Brad Smith: Of those animals that were more mobile, were they just moving from point A to point B or did they spend more time at sea or in Shelikof?

Peter Boveng: They actually spent some time out there. If you actually look at all locations you can see that they go out to an area, spend a little time, and then come back, typically. Once you get started looking at those poor quality locations; you have some of them that are just that, poor quality. The seal wasn't really there. You need to do some weeding, to do some fairly sophisticated filtering on those tracks to take in to account animal swim speeds, previous locations, and quality of individual locations to do a full reconstruction of the tracks to see how much time they spent in particular areas. That is one of the eventual objectives of the study.

Unidentified: You interpreted the ranging data in terms of inter-individual variability in foraging strategy. Has anyone looked at the diving data yet, time and depth data, to look at variation in dive patterns between those that are ranging way out and those that are staying around the haul out sites?

Peter Boveng: We haven't yet but that is a major objective. Data are still coming in. Incidentally, the dive data that we get from the satellite dive recorders is summarized in a histogram-type of data, but it still can be revealing about foraging patterns. That will be a primary analysis once we get some more of these tracks in hand.

John Petterson: How long does it take a seal to get from the west side down to Kodiak?

Peter Boveng: We can certainly tell that. I don't have all of those numbers at hand. I recall that one of those pups went from Chinitna Bay, down Augustine Island, and then down to the Douglas Reef area over the course of about three days.

AERIAL PHOTOGRAPHY OF BOWHEAD WHALES
TO ESTIMATE THE SIZE OF THE BERING-CHUKCHI-BEAUFORT POPULATION

Mr. David Rugh and Paul Wade, Ph.D.

National Marine Mammal Laboratory, Alaska Fisheries Science Center
7600 Sand Point Way NE, Seattle, WA 98115
(206) 526-4018, Fax (206) 526-6615, Email: dave.rugh@noaa.gov

Aerial photography is a proven technique for identifying many or most individual bowhead whales. Between 1976 and 2000, a total of 12,100 images of bowheads have been collected from aircraft flying directly over whales, mostly in the Beaufort Sea in summer and near Point Barrow during the spring migration. Most (10,366) of the bowhead images have been categorized as to photographic quality and degree of markings on the whales, and 7,813 of the images have been measured for length. Research groups have contributed to the database include LGL Limited, environmental research associates (LGL); the National Marine Mammal Laboratory (NMML); Cascadia Research Collective (CRC), and the North Slope Borough (NSB).

In 2003 and 2004 dedicated aerial photographic surveys were conducted by LGL during the bowhead spring migration past Point Barrow. This provided 1,150 photographs in 2003 and 1,443 in 2004, which is the best sampling we have yet for the full migration. To date, all of the photographs have been developed and labeled, and many images have been scanned in, but it will take considerable work before we can establish the sample size of good quality images with adequately marked whales. This is a critical step before abundance analyses can proceed.

Past studies have used results from the photographic data to estimate abundance, survival rates, growth rates, calving intervals, and length-frequency distribution. For instance, comparisons of images from spring 1985 (n = 641), summer 1985 (n = 1,069), spring 1986 (n = 401), and summer 1986 (n = 441) were used to make abundance estimates (DaSilva et al. 2000). Various statistical tests provided estimates with most likely values near 6,700, which is close to estimates from the ice-based counts in 1985 (6,039; 95% CI 3,300 - 11,100) and 1986 (7,734; 95% 5,400 - 11,100). The aerial photography approach to estimating abundance is less sensitive to vagaries in ice cover (a problem which is being accentuated with global warming, resulting in more fragile ice on which to establish counting stations), yet both methods (aerial photography and ice-based census) provide estimates with similar precision: SE = 1,696 - 2,017 for photographic results in 1985 and 1986, and SE = 1,450 - 1,915 for ice-based results in the same years.

The most recent abundance estimate, using systematic whale counts made at ice-based sites near Point Barrow in 2001, was 10,470 (95% CI = 8,100 to 13,500) with a rate of increase of 3.4% (95% CI = 1.7% to 5%) for the period 1978-2001 (George et al. 2004). Although this stock is currently listed as endangered under the Endangered Species Act, the status of this listing may need to be reevaluated, especially if there is continued evidence of an increase in abundance. Analyses of aerial photographs of bowheads may play a significant role in making these management decisions.

Literature Cited:

Da Silva, C.Q., J. Zeh, D. Madigan, J. Laake, D. Rugh, L Baraff, W Koski, and G. Miller. 2000. Capture-recapture estimation of bowhead whale population size using photo-identification data. Journal of Cetacean Research and Management 2(1):45-61.

George, J.C., J. Zeh, R. Suydam, and C. Clark. 2004. Abundance and population tread (1978-2001) of western Arctic bowhead whales surveyed near Barrow, Alaska. Marine Mammal Science 20(4):755-773.

Discussion:

Tom Newbury: I am surprised that there isn't any evidence that a particular group of animals, larger older animals, lead the migration especially beyond Barrow.

David Rugh: Eskimos describe whale leaders and I have seen it too from Cape Lisburne on a cliff. I watched one whale go by and then for hours others would follow. And yet the early part of the migration seems to be young whales. It is not like a very old mom will set the course and the rest of the migration follows. Robert Suydam do you have any other insights on that?

Robert Suydam: I agree that it is predominantly the young animals come through first. Whether the first whale that passes is a large whale or a small whale, who knows? I have heard certainly from various hunters that sometimes some of the big whales are actually the leaders and the young ones follow. But we predominantly see small animals in the first group that comes through in the spring.

Cleve Cowles: I am glad you spared us some of the statistical nuances of mark and recapture analysis that is your fundamental approach. In thinking about the assumptions and ramifications as I recall them, the aircraft from which you are photographing your sampling or recaptures, the ice-based camps, and the combined ice observations and acoustic approach for the traditional census approach, ultimately you are going to need to demonstrate comparability between the aircraft sampling and that. Then that brings to mind the question of aircraft surveys, which have their problems with weather and sea state, etc. Are you including adjustments for those variations in sampling to make the statistics comparable? I am curious whether you get into that level of refinement.

David Rugh: A lot of it has to do with sample size. As the years go by, and more photos are collected, then we can "tear it apart." For instance, I showed you two samples from Barrow and two samples from the Beaufort that were used in a variety of analyses to look at abundance estimates. Maybe you shouldn't compare Barrow with Beaufort if those are not completely the same populations. There are some theories that whales may come from the other side, such as Hudson Bay. Or maybe some whales get around Barrow far to the north. The Barrow-to-Barrow sampling would be the most appropriate mark and recapture for abundance at Barrow. Incidentally, there is an effort that is designed to start in April to fly around St. Lawrence Island and capture photographs. We'll compare Barrow to Barrow, Barrow to Beaufort, Barrow to St. Lawrence Island, and ask "Are these ratios different?" That may be a hint at a stock that doesn't go to Barrow if the resighting rate is much lower. But again there are a lot of ways of teasing the data apart. For instance, you can do an entire mark and recapture analysis on rostrums only, or midbacks only. Or you can do various combinations. That is why the project has only just begun and we are turning to the University of Washington with their expertise to refine that.

Bill Streever: I am intrigued by rumors for over two years about delisting the bowhead whale. I don't understand what would drive that? Why put the effort in and take the political heat of delisting such a charismatic animal, what is to be gained by delisting?

David Rugh: Part of it is for truth and accuracy. There are some species out there, some stocks who are truly endangered, who need the priority. If we have a species that is healthy and by all definitions in the Marine Mammal Protection Act and the Endangered Species Act, it is not at risk then we should take it off the list. But the incentive for that, that is a good point. It took us a decade or more to get gray whales off the list. From the time we started looking at the issue and realizing the numbers were high and rising, to the time we got them off the list, the abundance had doubled. But there is a lack of a driver there. Sometimes it is a lawsuit. When we get sued and we move faster. In the case of bowheads, we actually started the mechanism several years back and then put the brakes until the International Whaling Commission finished an intensive assessment. It may go on the shelf until we sort out the stock issues. What if there is a very small stock hidden amongst the big stock that is migrating northern Alaska? Or what if there is a substock in the Bering Sea or Chukchi Sea in the summer that 1s not seen at Barrow? That could elevate this whole issue of endangered animals.

Brad Smith: Is anyone looking at these photos for any index of health or condition? Something that might infer about not only the feeding habitats but long-term …?

David Rugh: We started into that a few years ago as an assessment, but these are black whales in very black water. You can't get the girth very easily. But we think our techniques are improving. I believe that Andrew Davis working with LGL potentially will be doing a doctoral study looking at girth. Now it has been done with gray whales. Wayne Perryman has shown that he can recognize a pregnant animal versus non-pregnant. In the event of 1999 and 2000 when hundreds of gray whales were dying on the beaches, he was able to say that these whales coming south were thinner than usual. You could actually see the pelvic bones and their backbones because they were so thin. It is a handle we can use, but sample size is the issue. How many times can you get a good girth?

John Richardson: During the bowhead feedings study a few years back, we attempted to measure girth to length ratios in bowheads from spring versus fall photos to see whether they were gaining or losing weight over the course of the summer. Only a small proportion of the photos are suitable from measuring girth. On average, the girth was greater when whales were leaving the Beaufort in the fall than for whales arriving in the spring (See Thomson 2002, Chapter 22 *in* OCS Study MMS 2002-012).

Literature Cited:

Thomson, D.H. 2002. Energetics of bowhead whales. Pages 22-1 to 22-40 (Chap. 22) *in* W.J. Richardson and D.H. Thomson (eds.), Bowhead whale feeding in the eastern Alaskan Beaufort Sea: update of scientific and traditional information, vol. 2. OCS Study MMS 2002-012; LGL Rep. TA2196-7. Rep. from LGL Ltd., King City, Ont. for U.S. Minerals Management Service, Anchorage, AK and Herndon, VA. 277p.

Discussion from the Barrow IUM:

Craig George: With all that scoring, what does the dataset looks like?

David Rugh: Yes that is a good point. You don't have to have all of them show to be used as a sample. Just the rostrums can be used in the mark and recapture or just midbacks. So they can almost be treated as independent.

Another thing that I didn't mention are the composites. As we are looking within a season, if we have one beautiful picture of the rostrum of a whale and another beautiful picture of its back, but the head is down, and there is just enough between the two pictures to recognize that it is the same whale, you can put this rostrum and this back together into a composite and you have more to work with. Now that resulting picture has a better chance of being found in another year. It increases the sample size when you have the option of working with composites.

Craig George: It makes the analysis complicated.

David Rugh: It does. It increases options, but it is a complicated process.

Social Science and Economics

QUANTITATIVE DESCRIPTION OF POTENTIAL IMPACTS OF OCS ACTIVITIES ON BOWHEAD WHALE HUNTING AND SUBSISTENCE ACTIVITIES IN THE BEAUFORT SEA

Michael A. Downs[1] and Barbara Bamberger[1]
John C. Russell[2], Michael Galginaitis[3], Don Schug[4], David Maas and Carl Shepro[5], Anne Jensen[6]

[1]EDAW Inc. 1420 Kettner Blvd, San Diego CA 92101
(619) 233-1454, FAX (619) 233-0952, Email: downsm@edaw.com, bambergerb@edaw.com;
[2]Adams-Russell Consulting, Email: john@adams-russell.com;
[3]Applied Sociocultural Research, Email: msgalginaitis@alaska.net;
[4] Northern Economics, Email: don.schug@norecom.com,
[5]Circumpolar Research Associates, Email: djmaas@comcast.net and afces1@uaa.alaska.edu,
[6] Ukpeagvik Iñupiat Corporation, Email: anne.jensen@uicscience.org

Subsistence hunting for marine mammals and especially bowhead whales has a long history as an organizing element of Iñupiat social, cultural, religious, and economic life. Oil development in general over the past 40 years has been associated with broad changes in Iñupiat communities: new sociopolitical institutions emerged, settlement and residence patterns changed, and new technologies became increasingly available. Perceptions of change varied, but OCS oil activities were perceived to present unique threats and consequences, including ones specific to whaling. Concerns have been expressed that OCS oil development activities could deflect whale migration farther off-shore, contribute to whale skittishness, and otherwise adversely affect whale behavior. Given the central nature of whaling in cultural and social organization, any threats to whaling are also seen as affecting other aspects of community and personal life. The purpose of the study is to document and analyze the perceptions of North Slope residents regarding historical, current, and potential future effects of oil industry activities on whales and whale hunting, associated social practices, and local society in general. This study has involved ethnographic fieldwork in Barrow, Nuiqsut, and Kaktovik on the North Slope, as well as in Savoonga, a Yu'pik village on Saint Lawrence Island that is serving as a contrastive case study.

This study was initiated in 2002 when the team developed the original research design and associated research protocols. A literature review detailing OCS development on the North Slope and its effects on Iñupiat culture and bowhead whaling activities has been completed, as has fieldwork in the four participating communities. In-field data collection, including implementation of the surveys and ethnographic interviews, occurred from March through October 2004. To obtain a representative sampling of opinions and perceptions, three separate survey instruments were developed and implemented in each of the four villages. The surveys were targeted to obtain the observations and opinions of Iñupiat and Yu'pik individual households, whaling captains, and youth, with regard to whaling, development, and OCS activity. Over 550 residents participated in the household survey, 125 residents participated in the whaling captain survey, and 50 students participated in the youth survey. To put the survey data in context, the study team also developed a protocol for qualitatively oriented ethnographic interviews of 50+ village leaders, participatory meetings, and a gender-inclusive approach to community workshops. Team members met with community elders, elected officials, whaling captains' wives associations, Arctic Slope Regional Corporation board members, local Native Corporation representatives, other local institutional representatives, and whaling crewmembers. Interviews and surveys together resulted in over 700 individuals participating in the four villages.

Survey data have been entered into a customized database, statistical analysis is ongoing, and sections of the draft report are in preparation. The draft report is scheduled for public review in the summer of 2005. The report will present an analysis of perceived cultural and social impacts of oil exploration/production on the Iñupiat subsistence way of life; the economic effects of development on employment, unemployment, and household living income; and perspectives on social and political changes in the communities studied. The report will include a statistical analysis measuring the prevalence and distribution of residents' concerns about OCS activity, as well as address the variation of opinion among different member-groups within the communities, with regard to beneficial and detrimental effects of OCS activities as they relate to bowhead whaling. Finally, the report will address lessons learned, including any unanticipated constraints and challenges involved with conducting this study; recommendations resulting from these lessons, to aide future studies; and suggestions for future studies.

Discussion:

Mike Burwell: Can you explain further about the student participation?

Michael Downs: I will ask Michael Galginaitis, one of the study team members to help out on this. But it just proved to be more difficult than we had anticipated to ... well let me back up for a minute. First of all the universe [of students potentially available to participate] is small. So in Nuiqsut and Kaktovik, I can't remember off the top of my head, but in terms of the numbers of, we were looking at juniors and seniors, the combined total was about ten students.

Michael Galginaitis: It was difficult to engage students in that age group. There was resistance to answering those questions. We also needed to get parental consent. So essentially we had to get consent from two people for each student surveyed: from the adults and the student. There were cases where a student would want to participate but the adult would not allow it. So that was an additional factor that went in to why we had a low response rate.

Michael Downs: And those start to add up when you have a universe that is small to begin with.

Jim Bennett: If I understand you correctly, this is a study essentially of perceptions, which is very valuable for MMS. Is there any reconciliation or treatment of how these perceptions reconcile with the facts?

Michael Downs: When you say reconciling with the facts, let's say the whaling captains suggest that there has been deflection as a result of specific events, are we going back as part of this study and looking at the record of barge activity? No, that is not part of the study design. The short answer is no, we are not going back and looking at the specific events. To the extent we can in the interviews, we are asking for specific events and for people to be as concrete as they can. As I understand it, a lot of that information doesn't exist in an accessible form that would allow us to consistently cross check that.

Jeff Childs: Relatively recently, in ecology, there has been the concept of shifting baselines. Is your analysis going to include breaking down the perceptions across generations as far as these changes?

Michael Downs: Yes. One of the things that the North Slope Borough was especially interested in, which was then incorporated into the study design, was change across generations in terms of perceptions of interactions with OCS but also in terms of rates of participation in whaling activities, subsistence, just intergenerational change along several dimensions. That was one of the things that the high school survey was intended to help us with. So we are a little bit handicapped for that generational shift. But as part of the household survey, there was a subset of surveys that were earmarked as elder surveys. And we do have age data so that we can look at differences between older generations. But we are missing the type of information to do the quantitative analysis that we would want to do, comparing the high school generation and then the next older generation. We can look at the older generations but we have a problem with the high school generation.

Brad Smith: This might by outside of your study area, I don't know if this is just for the Beaufort Sea communities or outside. But I know that the Point Lay and Shismaref and possibly other communities have expressed an interest in becoming whaling villages. I was wondering whether your study picked up on that type of an issue?

Michael Downs: No. It was just the Beaufort Sea that was called for in our study design; just the three communities from Barrow and east [Nuiqsut and Kaktovik], then Savoonga as a case study control community.

Bill Streever: I had a general question about studies like this and maybe specific to Barrow, as well or to the other villages too. It seems like in some of these groups you have people that have been interviewed for a lot of things repeatedly which is bit unusual for sociological studies. I am wondering, in general, how you deal with those kinds of situations? There are other places, like small villages in Asia, where this occurs. I wonder if there is a general protocol for doing that type of study? And if so, how is it being applied in the villages on the Slope?

Michael Downs: Let me see if I understand your question because I think there are two different parts to that. One is how do you get people to participate who have been interviewed many times? The second is what is the effect of being interviewed many times? This was a collaborative study from the beginning with the North Slope Borough and the AEWC. So there was some institutional inertia, for local institutions to assist in the study and to help us to communicate their local interest in the study. So to differentiate this a bit from some of the other studies that may have been perceived as coming from the outside with little or no local benefit, it really helped that the NSB and AEWC were actively communicating with the people and that they were a participant in this study. That collaboration extended to keeping those institutions and other local institutions apprised of the study throughout the process. So I think that helped. Obviously, that can be more effective in terms of whaling captains, for example, in getting the AEWC communicating with whaling captains to help participation rates than perhaps the AEWC or NSB communicating with high school age potential participants.

My second interpretation of your question is how does that affect results? Do things become routinized through asking the same things over time? One of the things that we have done is to go back and look at public testimony, look at previous public input, to see if there have been changes over time. The second thing is that where we felt that the ethnographic interview was important in terms of trying to get some context to help us in the interpretation of the survey results. To develop a richer context so that if we could elicit some nuances there that may not be obvious in the survey answers.

Rob Stapleton: You indicated that your field studies were done. I was wondering if you would consider or had any plans to revisit some of the villages where you got poor results from the teenagers? If not, why not? And if you would use a different methodology?

Michael Downs: Our initial surveys are completed. We are obviously open to additional attempts to gather information that we weren't able to gather in the first place. So, if there were cause or a reason to believe that that information could be gained, we certainly would talk to the study team at MMS and explore that. At this point, staying with the consistent methodology, comparability between surveys, I don't think we have any realistic expectations that we will be able to dramatically improve the response rates, maintaining a consistent approach across the different survey instruments.

In terms of going back to the communities, just as part of normal protocol, but especially because this is a collaborative effort, the draft findings will be discussed in each of the communities in the form of community presentations. I am sure along with that some key-person follow up. I do expect that there will be additional input once the initial findings are discussed. So I guess when I said that the fieldwork is done I meant the formal part of the fieldwork, in terms of the application of the survey instruments. But yes there will be additional community input before the report is finalized.

Steve Braund: I was very interested in hearing about your response from the high school students. I agree with everything you said, in terms of comparability. I have been in many of these villages doing MMS and non-MMS studies and a lot of mapping studies of subsistence. In the non-MMS projects that do not have the sampling restrictions and prescribed methodologies of who we select, I actually solicit 17, 18, 19 year olds, 20 year olds. I was particularly struck in the last two years in Nuiqsut by the high subsistence activity of these younger persons. I only bring this up because I don't want anyone in the audience to go home with the take-a-way message that the young people aren't participating in subsistence activities. I think it may be that they just didn't participate in your survey. I can understand reasons why. I think you are probably right on track with only seven, nine, or ten kids in school and you can't really go very far with that in terms of comparing results across communities. But at the same time, in the future, you might not just use high school, but stretch your sample to the 17 to 24 year old group. You would probably get different results, but maybe not in a survey situation.

Michael Downs: Thanks, Steve.

Dee Williams: I just want to add some additional comments to the discussion. I think it is fair to say that EDAW went to great effort to secure participation. Somethings that were left unsaid include monetary compensation even to the teenagers to further encourage them to participate. So there was not a minimal effort at all. We feel that we gave it the best effort we could to enhance participation.

Another point I wanted to comment on is the comparing perceptions to empirical facts. It is true that the study did not budget to task our contractor to exhaustively and systematically go back and explain all of the empirical data that MMS has collected over 30 years to put in contrast or in corroboration with local perceptions. There was not a systematic place to do that. But, however, I felt like perhaps you had the incorrect perception that there is no place at all for empirical findings to come out in the report by way of checking or validating the validity of the perceptions being recorded. That is going to happen. We are collecting the perceptions. In the places where it is possible and fairly easy to corroborate with empirical findings that is part of the task of the report. The contractors have specifically requested assistance in data from the Borough to provide for fairly simple empirical data about whale strikes for example, and other things that can fairly easily be used to verify and validate some of the perceptions that are being expressed. So it is not that there is no place for empiricism in the study.

Robert Suydam: Thank you for your final comments, Dee. Although, I would like caution the assumption that the empirical data are the truth or that they are fact. Many times hunters' perceptions have proven to be true when the empirical data weren't. So that assuming that empirical data are the truth is not necessarily a good way to go.

Dee Williams: Fair enough. I guess as a social scientist we assume that to be part of the trappings of our profession. It does bear saying in a public forum that the clarity of what is knowledge and what is factual is subject to interpretation.

Discussion from the Barrow IUM:

Doreen Simmons: Are the transcripts or tapes available?

Michael Downs: No, the interviews were not taped. The surveys were done one-on-one with a survey form. The individual surveys themselves are confidential but the compiled results of the surveys will be available. Frequencies of answers on questions and comments on the open ended questions will be available as part of the reporting process.

Doreen Simmons: Even anonymous information would be valuable for this community.

Michael Downs: Absolutely. Maybe I didn't' say that clearly enough. We are compiling the results, community by community, so that information will be available.

Tim Holder: You mentioned that on the high school survey you didn't have enough participation to be statistically valid. There were 52 respondents from Barrow and seven or eight from Nuiqsut and Kaktovik?

Michael Downs: There will still be some good information in terms of a qualitative discussion. But we will not be able to do the quantitative analysis, comparing and contrasting the high school survey with the other surveys that we had hoped to do.

Tim Holder: What would have been the thresholds?

Michael Downs: What would have been the threshold that we would have had to capture to do the quantitative analysis for the high school survey?

Michael Galginaitis: In Kaktovik, essentially sampling and interviewing resulted in seven or eight completed interviews.

Tim Holder: But for Barrow there was 52 and wouldn't that be enough?

Michael Galginaitis: I believe for Barrow that is adequate. But we could not differentiate among villages.

Michael Downs: One of the things that the Borough and the AEWC were interested in exploring was how does proximity to existing development influence things? Do you see different things in Nuiqsut than at Kaktovik? But we will be able to do things with the Barrow sampling.

Tim Holder: Is it too late to go back and expand the age range for the high school survey if MMS was interested in funding that?

Michael Downs: There is always more that you can do. But in terms of doing so within the parameters of the existing study design, with trying to maintain comparability between the surveys, trying to do it in a similar time frame, and retain your comparability within instruments, there are difficulties, but there is always more you can do. We can go back and get more information but realistically for this particular study, right now, I think that would work better as a follow up study than something that we could capture immediately.

Tim Holder: And try to make it look like it was integrated.

George Olemaun: On the socioeconomic studies, we have had one started on the impacts of oil and gas activities on the native population. Is your study different than that one?

Michael Downs: I'm not sure which study you mean. This was a study that originated two and a half years ago. So I don't know if it is the same one you are talking about.

George Olemaun: Well, we just started that one last year on the impacts of oil and gas activities within the North Slope on the native population.

Michael Downs: Our survey was conducted this last year from March through October. So that may be the same one you are talking about. It did have questions specifically on the effects of oil and gas activities.

There were questions about OCS activities in general, the economy in general. Then there was a section specifically on the interaction between whales and OCS activity. So it is likely that these are one and the same study.

Doreen Lampe: For OCS activities, does that include exploration and development? If so, what type of exploration and development would you actually conduct during what parts of the year? The entire area?

Michael Downs: Yes. Our study was asking people about their perceptions of the impacts of activities. I can't speak for the timing of the activities themselves.

Doreen Lampe: So it practically all of the proposed OCS development impacts?

I noticed that a lot of people hardly attend these meetings any more. They are so frustrated with the way meetings are set up and the statistics that are used to say it is safe to develop in the Arctic. But there is really no proven oil spill clean up program. There is none. When you are thinking about proceeding with oil and gas development, all of the activity, look at the impact here. It is like people have given up. There is no communication. There is a study on communication. What does it have to take to get you to understand that it (development) should not occur? Everyone talks about studies and that they are all healthy right now. We know that. But the event of oil spill, there is no plan. There is none, zero. But yet you proceed with "look at all of our studies, they show it is good." But in reality, at one planning commission meeting, an oil company said that they will be developing in winter and if there were an oil spill, the oil would move as slow as molasses. That was their response. So what if it moves as slow as molasses? You'll be moving even slower in – 50 degree weather trying to clean up that spill.

Why aren't you sponsoring some kind of program for universities to test the best method of cleaning up oil spills or something like that? I just don't understand. What is it going to take to let you know that we oppose offshore drilling and that there is no proven technology for oil spill clean up? It is an impact to the people. You come and say we did this, we did that, and we did this, etc. But still you have no ability to clean up an oil spill in the Arctic. None.

Dick Prentki: I would like to respond a couple of the questions you asked. Before any oil structure would be allowed to be developed, such as at Northstar and at Liberty, they would have to have an oil spill contingency plan. So there would be a response plan as part of their planning requirements. Now that doesn't address the success of that plan. But they would have to have one. It would have to be approved by the MMS and the U. S. Coast Guard.

In terms of putting money out to try and improve oil spill response and clean up capabilities, MMS does that. We have a major program, the Technology Assessment and Research branch, that is out of our headquarters unit. We have a big wave tank facility in New Jersey where we actually add ice and do ice experiments and test clean up equipment in ice conditions. In the Alaska region this year we started a fairly large study to get more information on how oil moves or doesn't move with the ice, depending upon specific oil chemistry and weather conditions. So we are doing something. We may not have all of the answers but we are trying.

Tim Holder: I think also there is the perception of the risks. Can you ever get the risks down to zero if you are working with oil structures? From an engineering standpoint, I don't think you could ever get to zero, as I understand it. But there are many measures that can be taken. It is part of MMS's responsibility as steward of the resources to minimize that risk and get it as close to zero as possible.

As an example, with the Northstar project, it sits on a gravel island about nine miles offshore. The oil is drilled from below the sea floor and is brought up to the gravel island. Then there is a pipeline that is about 20 ft below the sea floor that takes the oil to the shoreline to the pipeline infrastructure onshore. The reason that it is 20 ft below the sea floor is that was gauged to be the level below which there would be ice gouging. So that is one engineering element to reduce that part of the risk.

There is also an extensive amount of engineering that went in to the design of the pipeline to make sure it wouldn't rupture and corrode.

There is also a system to detect any leaking from the pipeline itself. As I understand it, the system is set up so that if there were a leak from the pipeline, there would be an immediate shut down. So there would be a rather minimal amount of leakage from the system.

So in the case of the first offshore oil development, those are some of the things being done to minimize the risk of oil spills. Also, I think as a parallel example, in the Gulf of Mexico where there is extensive offshore oil development that is under the jurisdiction of the MMS, the amount of spills from pipelines in the Gulf of Mexico is very low.

Dick Prentki: It is probably on the order of a fraction of a spill per billion barrels produced. On Liberty, we are talking about 100 million barrels. It is not zero, but the probability of a spill would be like one to two percent from a long pipeline. Those calculations need to be done in a proper fashion rather than try to give a number now.

That would be a part of the analysis that they would do for the environmental impact statement and report if Liberty proceeds. And look at differences between risks from pipeline spills in the Arctic environment versus what they would have in the Gulf of Mexico and take in to account ice gouging, etc. But you can't get it to zero.

Tim Holder: I don't want to imply that the Arctic is the same as the Gulf of Mexico. There are obviously many more challenges in the Arctic than in the gulf due to the challenging environment. I know this doesn't answer all of your questions. But just to let you know that there are a lot of efforts and thought behind some of the studies to minimize the risk of oil spills.

Craig George: To follow up on what Doreen asked, I have watched these meetings for many years. I think that what the frustration is in the community, and maybe some of the older folks for whom English is a second language, is that they consistently say that they don't want oil development. But I think what people would like to hear is an honest response. "Well we understand that, but it is going ahead anyway." Or whatever. That is, I think, the disconnect here. The community has spoken and said that they don't want it. But it won't go away. Why is that?

Did you ask in the survey whether people were for or against offshore development?

Michael Downs: As a specific question, for or against offshore development?

Michael Galginaitis: We did ask if they thought it was possible to do oil development in an environmentally responsible way. But we didn't ask if they liked it or not.

Craig George: Did I make it clear what is the basis for their frustration? I am just wondering if MMS owes the community a frank answer, like "Sorry, this is driven by national politics. We are here and we are going to try and develop. And that is the bottom line. So regardless of what comments are made we have to do this." So maybe that is what needs to be stated if that is the truth. I don't know what the truth is.

Tim Holder: I have been with MMS since 1988 and have known about it since 1981 when I worked with the City of Nome and followed oil and gas leasing offshore of Nome and Norton Sound. I think what happens is that MMS is part of a large bureaucracy within the Department of the Interior. There is this elaborate process of writing environmental impact statements, holding public meetings, and going through all of these exercises for the last thirty years. People do get tired and fatigued hearing the same answers especially if they are really against offshore oil development. I think that the disconnect is that the people that come to the meetings who represent MMS are relatively lower level staff people. The people who ultimately make the decisions about holding a lease sale is the Secretary of the Interior. Since the 1970s, this has gone through both Democratic and Republican administrations and administrations that have leaned toward protecting the environment and those that have been rather bullish on developing the offshore. Yet it is sort of like the ship that keeps sailing forward on a steady course. When you look at what happens at the local level and what the local people are saying it seems to get lost in the shuffle by the time it gets up to whoever is the Secretary of Interior and whoever is sitting in the White House. Part of it is that they are considered national resources. So whoever occupies those positions is looking at it from a national level. So it can be very frustrating being at the local level especially here on the North Slope where people rely on subsistence resources, especially bowhead whale hunting. If an oil spill happened that affected the bowhead whaling, it would be a huge disaster for the community. Not just the lost of the meat and the sustenance, but a disastrous effect for the culture. I know that doesn't answer or alleviate the frustration but I think that is an explanation of how the process works and how I have watched it happen.

Craig George: So what is the message to people who come to meetings year after year? Well, is it keep on coming and saying the same thing and we'll write it down? Or will it make a difference?

Dick Prentki: Yes, keep on doing it. It gets very frustrating for us too. We have a five-year plan. Every five years we start all over. If something was settled in the last five-year plan, it is open game again. Within the five-year plan, we may have two or three sales offered in the Beaufort. The way it usually works is that if we decide at the first sale we won't offer something because we agreed that there is too much risk involved, it will get reconsidered again two years down the line at the next sale. That is the way the system is set up.

So, please don't stop. Keep coming to meetings.

Doreen Lampe: When I was listening to some of these reports, some of the populations like ducks decreased and the cause is unknown. The fish declined and the cause is unknown. They thought the whales were extinct but you are proving that they are on the rise. Every time when something happens to a population of animals, we are the first to be blamed not the oil industry, not the government. We have to take the fall for the industry, for the government. We have to pay the price not the government, not the oil industry. Yet you still have all of these programs, make these laws, allow oil development and say it is all fine and good. But when something goes wrong, it will be the Natives' fault. You will want us to quit duck hunting, quit fishing, or quit whaling.

Michael Elauqak: I am a native allotment owner at the Teshekpuk area. I would like to know if you did an ice study in that area? If there is a blow out there, ice and oil don't mix. Was the migratory path of the whales studied? What is going to happen if there is an oil spill out there? This is not Cook Inlet; this is the Beaufort. You have to let the whole community know, not just the agencies. You have to let everyone know. My concern is about the ice conditions. If you have a blowout, once there is an oil spill, that piece of ice is going to travel all over. It is going to affect all of the animals.

Dick Prentki: MMS does spend a lot of time trying to figure out what will happen to that oiled ice. We take oceanography measurements, current measurements. We try to model events. We are working very hard on that issue. Our models aren't perfect. But we are spending a lot of time and efforts trying to work on that. It is a concern for us and we are trying to work on that.

Michael Elauqak: What about the studies of the ice conditions in that area?

Dick Prentki: We have studies looking at the circulation of the water under the ice right now. Current meters are moored out there under the ice. We have a major study that is trying to develop a better ice model to look at local movements of ice. We have another study that is trying to better figure out movement of ice in the landfast ice zone, so when it does move, or when it forms and breaks up. Each crude oil is different and behaves differently. We are trying to figure out how each crude oil behaves in ice and snow and movement under the ice. We are trying to work on those problems. It is not easy.

Doreen Simmons: I have a question about communications. I work at KBRW and, for I don't know how many meetings since I have been there, whether it is BLM or MMS, you don't call early enough to get these kinds of meetings aired. I understand that the request to have this meeting live was asked only two days ago. That is not enough time. It is common sense: ask early enough for something like this. Two days is not enough. So KBRW had to say no. People like Doreen Lampe have to be heard. This is not getting out to the public.

Also, along the same lines as Doreen, I think in metaphors... MMS comes and says this is what we are going to do. All this has happened in the past too. It is like someone coming into your house and saying we are doing something that is going to make money. It is going to make a lot of noise and it may damage your eardrums, it may damage your body, but we'll get you some earplugs. That is not enough. It is not working. It is just common sense. We all know that it is going to be very dangerous.

Tim Holder: Thank you. Just to follow up a little bit, I would like to add on to what Dick said. Even though it has been decades and people get very tired about reiterating and responding to the same issues, etc., it does help to hear what the concerns are. This process is really set up under the National Environmental Policy Act (NEPA), which in its own way does have a lot of things that work. There are a lot of stipulations that have been put into lease sales that are basically environmental safeguards. There is a lot of consultation with important stakeholders, including, in this case, the North Slope Borough. There has been, in the last year and a half, letters exchanged between the mayor of the Borough and MMS to iron out some important issues concerning upcoming lease sale in the Beaufort Sea. These processes take a long time and take a lot of energy. I don't even go to my community council meetings about issues going on in my neighborhood. I know that you live in an area with a relatively small population which huge issues. I can only imagine how worn out people up here get going to all of the meetings. Even though you have some really good staff, professional biologists, etc. to help articulate your issues and respond, it is still an exhaustive process.

Yet I encourage you to keep on working with us and we'll do our best to respond.

THE NORTH SLOPE ECONOMY: 1965 TO PRESENT

Leah Cuyno, Ph.D.

Northern Economics, Inc., 880 H Street, Suite 210, Anchorage, AK 99501
(907) 274-5600, Fax (907) 274-5601, E-Mail: Leah.Cuyno@norecon.com

Information from this historical perspective on the evolution of the North Slope economy will be useful to MMS in assessing potential economic impacts of OCS development activity on the North Slope and its residents. The study explores the structural changes that had significant economic, institutional, and social impacts on the region. In the first phase of the study these structural changes were reviewed with respect to:

- *The changes in employment and economic activities of the region.*

Prior to 1968, employment opportunities on the North Slope were primarily limited to federal and state activities, and North Slope villages could only afford limited local government. The discovery of oil in Prudhoe Bay in 1968, formation of the regional and village corporations after passage of the ANCSA in 1971, and formation of the North Slope Borough (NSB) in 1972 dramatically changed the physical and economic infrastructure of the region. These events created a more diverse economy with increased activities in construction, oil and gas extraction, and support sectors such as transportation, communications, and utilities (TCU), and other service sectors. While employment and total earnings in the region increased significantly, the wealth created (from net earnings) did not necessarily create significant effects in the regional economy, as most of these dollars were earned by non-residents and were not re-spent in the regional economy.

- *The role of local governments.*

Through its ability to levy taxes on oil and gas properties within the Borough, the NSB has provided employment and services to all North Slope communities and has been the largest employer of North Slope Iñupiat. The NSB has financed its operating expenditures and debt service primarily with property tax revenues. It has financed virtually all of its capital expenditures with general obligation bonds. As the oil and gas production and pipeline property depreciates, the tax revenues to the Borough have declined. The declining revenues are causing significant budgetary challenges, leading to reductions in the scale of capital projects.

- *The role of the Arctic Slope Regional Corporation (ASRC) and village for-profit corporations.*

ASRC and the eight village corporations have been a significant economic force in the region, providing jobs to residents and opportunities to be involved in all sectors of the economy (i.e., construction, oilfield activities, retail and service sector, etc.). Since 1973, the ASRC has increased its revenues at an average rate of 39 percent per year. In 2003, the corporation's gross revenues amounted to about $1 billion. Both the ASRC and village corporations have served as vehicles to channel Native assets and capital toward productive investments on behalf of their shareholders. While they are required by law to make good faith efforts at earning financial returns for their shareholders, they also put emphasis on hiring their shareholders, providing for educational needs of their shareholders and children, and are also involved in political and social issues.

- *Individual and household economic response to changes.*

The substantial expansion of public facilities and services that has occurred in North Slope communities over the past twenty-five years has significantly improved the quality of village life. Significant improvements have occurred in water and sanitation facilities, health and social services, education, housing, public safety, transportation and communication. While long-standing income inequalities between Iñupiat and non-Iñupiat households continue, income increases among Iñupiat households appear to be fairly evenly distributed. To some extent, the income increases experienced by North Slope households have been offset by the high cost of living. Surveys indicate that subsistence resources continue to be of economic and cultural importance to residents, although the adoption of modern technology has raised the cost of participating in subsistence activities. While North Slope residents generally agree that the overall quality of life in their communities has improved, they continue to express concern about the social effects of rapid economic development in the region.

A second phase of the study, which is in-progress, examines 1) the historical function of non-profit Native corporations, tribal governments, and the Federal and State governments in the North Slope economy and 2) the linkages among the various public and private entities that have played a major role in the regional economy.

Discussion:

Tom Newbury: I liked your list of significant factors on the North Slope Borough, like the discovery of oil. You listed peak production, but the prices varied so much, wouldn't it make more sense to list the peak oil income? In other words, to multiply the volume that is produced by the price? In 1988, it probably wasn't peak income. The price of oil was much higher 1978, 1980, and is much higher now that was in 1988.

Leah Cuyno: Yes, I need to check that. It might have been the peak oil production.

Nancy Mundy: The price of oil has a lot bigger implication for the State of Alaska than for the North Slope Boroughs. The North Slope Borough's income is tied to property values. They don't get a bonanza when the price goes up.

Ben Greene: You rather vaguely alluded to some sentiments on behalf the North Slope Borough residents that they felt that their quality of life was higher than it "used to be." Is there any way to quantify that? Is there anything more than just anecdotal statements?

Leah Cuyno: Yes, in our report we go into much detail about the educational attainment, provision of public utilities, income, and all of those other quality of life indicators that I listed.

Ben Greene: Yet attainment of education, those things that you just mentioned, are perhaps more western values. I hope on that list of indicators you have some categories that are more closely aligned with traditional subsistence people's values as well. It is difficult to do.

Leah Cuyno: Yes, we do have a section on subsistence and how the way of doing subsistence activities has changed through the years due to technology factors.

Bill Streever: You had two slides: one that showed revenues and one that showed expenses. The revenue chart had the revenues from the oil industry and you mentioned that that kind of mirrored the debt service revenue. But it also looked to me that at some point those two lines are going to cross. If that was my household finance statement, I would be worried. Is there a projection of when those lines are going to cross?

Leah Cuyno: We have that in the report. We talk about the budgetary challenges. We have one chart that merges those two graphs. I can't remember when those two lines will cross. We actually relegated that section to the back of that section. We are in the process of rewriting that section. We actually received some strong reaction from the Borough. So we are going to rework that section.

Rex Okakok, Sr.: Do you have any statistics that show how much Federal money received since 1965 to date? That is not oil related but it is related to impacts. If we didn't have those Federal money then we wouldn't have those impacts. The only reason we have those monies coming in from the Federal government is because we have to deal with health impacts, education.

Leah Cuyno: This topic is actually being handled in the second phase of the report. We already collected information from the Consolidated Federal Funds Report (CFFR) that shows how much Federal dollars are flowing into each of the regions in the State. We have that data collected already.

Nancy Mundy: That is one of the reasons we want to look at the nonprofit native groups in the Borough also. Because a lot of that money, now instead of the Federal government spending it directly in the Borough, it is being funneled through Alaska native nonprofits. They are taking care of health and some of the other issues and managing them.

Rex Okakok, Sr.: The North Slope Borough gets contracts with the Federal government to respond to social needs, health care, etc. Is that separated from revenues?

Leah Cuyno: In the Federal expenditures? Yes the different programs are separated out.

Bill Streever: Did you have any projections for how a gas pipeline might affect the formula?

Leah Cuyno: We are doing that for a different project. Employment will increase.

Bill Streever: Does it take us back to the "glory days" or is it just a small blip?

Leah Cuyno: I don't know right now.

Tim Holder: The charge to the consultants on this project was to look at the baseline economy from 1965 to the present. They actually did some forecast information that was above and beyond the original scope.

Leah Cuyno: We weren't supposed to look at the oil and gas issues.

Tim Holder: It was basically to look at the communities of the North Slope Borough as separate from the oil patch where the workers basically take their money back away from the Borough. We have a separate set of models that deal with projecting employment and income.

Rex Okakok, Sr.: It would be interesting to see how the Federal dollars when they started coming in, how they grew and then stabilized. I think that alone will show the impact that industry has had among our Iñupiat people.

Leah Cuyno: I will try to pull up that slide before the trip to Barrow and show it when we are there at the Information Update Meeting.

Celeste Rueffert: You had a couple of slides that talked about the increase in income and the decrease in the poverty level. How does that compare with the State overall or nationally? Did you do any comparisons?

Leah Cuyno: I think, in terms of real income, most of the State actually has not increased that much. It is certainly not in that magnitude. I am not sure about the poverty level. Do you know Nan?

Nancy Mundy: The poverty level is fairly low, similar to the State. But it doesn't take into account any of the differences in cost of living across places. So it is really hard to compare people living in Anchorage with people living in Barrow where things cost so much more.

Discussion from the Barrow IUM:

Craig George: Can you go back to the graph showing "debt return"?

Tim Holder: That graph looks a little funny. Part of the reason that the lines are not continuous is that there was missing data.

Leah Cuyno: There was some missing data.

Dick Prentki: Did they use bonds to finance those?

Craig George: Yes. A lot of the things you see, housing, clinics, fire halls, utilidor, happened in the early 1980s. But now the capital projects... so the Borough income is not shown on that graph? Correct?

Leah Cuyno: No it is not on this slide. We have a chart in the report that will show these two lines together, and they intersect at some point.

Craig George: That is what I was wondering, where those two lines are going to intersect. So basically all of the income is going to pay for maintenance, debt, etc.

Leah Cuyno: There was one year where 60% of the operating budget went to debt retirement.

Doreen Simmons: Can we get copies of the report?

Leah Cuyno: There is a draft report out. We are addressing all of the comments now. But this power point presentation can be made available.

Tim Holder: The draft report is being reviewed by MMS. The final report is due in July.

Leah Cuyno: I have a hard copy of the presentation with me.

Craig George: I was surprised that in the 1950s the median income was $20,000 that seems relatively high.

Leah Cuyno: This is in 2001 dollars.

Tim Holder: So in 1959 dollars, it was probably half of that, maybe about $10,000.

Craig George: So that is all adjusted to current values. The cost of living here has always been high.

Leah Cuyno: That is correct. This actually compares with the rest of the country and Alaska. But if you consider cost of living, it is a different story.

David Rugh: Was subsistence included?

Leah Cuyno: No.

Craig George: So you call "subsistence" an economy, I am not used to that. No one makes any money from it.

Leah Cuyno: Some researchers try to quantify the value of non-cash economy, the time involved, the money involved.

RESEARCHING TECHNICAL DIALOGUE WITH ALASKAN COASTAL COMMUNITIES: ANALYSIS OF THE SOCIAL, CULTURAL, LINGUISTIC, AND INSTITUTIONAL PARAMETERS OF PUBLIC/AGENCY COMMUNICATION PATTERNS

Michael A. Downs and Barbara Bamberger[1] Michael Galginaitis[2], Sarah Barton[3], Patrick Burden and Nancy Mundy[4], Ron Scollon[5], Joe Jorgensen[6], Chase Hensel[7]

[1]EDAW Inc. 1420 Kettner Blvd, San Diego CA 92101
(619) 233.1454 Fax (619) 233-0952, Email: downsm@edaw.com, bambergerb@edaw.com;
[2]Applied Sociocultural Research, Email: msgalginaitis@alaska.net;
[3]Rise Alaska, Email: sbarton@risealaska.com;
[4] Northern Economics, Email: patrick.burden@norecon.com, nancy.mundy@norecon.com;
[5]Georgetown University, Linguistics Department, Email: scollonr@georgetown.edu;
[6] University of California-Irvine, Anthropology Department, Email: jjorgens@comcast.net;
[7]Morrow and Hensel Consulting, Email: ffch@uaf.edu

The primary goal of this MMS Study is to evaluate and facilitate improvements in technical dialogue with stakeholders in Alaska OCS regions, particularly with populations of concern. Technical dialogue, for the purpose of this study, has been defined as two-way written communications between the public agency and the communities affected by public policy. This study will investigate the effects and dynamics of written communication efforts by MMS in the North Slope and Cook Inlet planning areas. The study will also explore possible remedies to communication difficulties through pilot-testing a series of experimental newsletters on targeted focus groups. If significant communication obstacles can be identified and reduced through controlled testing, recommendations will be made to help shape future agency interactions with the public. In its management role, MMS has the task of trying to communicate complex ideas, plans, and supporting documentation for a variety of projects and improving the communication process would help coastal communities to participate more fully in the NEPA project decision-making process.

This study will, in part, analyze how different stakeholders view the effectiveness of MMS communication with the public in North Slope and Cook Inlet communities, legitimacy of the MMS public participation process itself, accuracy of the MMS technical dialogue, how risk is interpreted in Native and non-Native communities (with regard to OCS activity), and the patterns and problems associated with inter-cultural communication between agency staff and community stakeholders. The study approach utilizes communication theory; deliberative public participation models; and an ethnographic approach to understanding of both Native and non-Native communities in the two regions that include a range of social and linguistic particularities, energy development histories, and regional economic foundations. A literature review of public communication processes, which includes a comparison of technical and public communication models from the USFS, NPS, and other federal agencies, is in process as is a socio-linguistic analysis of MMS records of public testimony and EIS written communication with regard to OCS activity. The purpose of analyzing these records is to untangle messages found in the respondents' written communication, and to identify messages to test in the North Slope and Cook Inlet communities. A consideration of regional differences in views of the natural environment and perceptions of the relationship between science-based and tradition-based ecological knowledge will figure in the analysis of interpretation and perception of accurate technical dialogue. This analysis will draw specifically on the fields of anthropology, ethnolinguistics, socio-economics, and public communication.

In addition to the literature review(s) and agency communication model evaluation, the multi-method approach utilized for this study will include interviews with MMS staff to provide an internal institutional history and perspective, stakeholder focus group meetings, and limited key person interviews. This study is in the early stages, and the focus group design and associated protocols are currently being formulated. Focus group meetings in each region to provide a baseline of existing understandings and issues and to test new materials are anticipated to take place in the fall/winter of 2005/6. Findings and recommendations will be documented in a report to be completed in 2006.

Discussion:

Rex Okakok, Sr.: I am always concerned about how we define communication and try to come up with some way to communicate two ways. I have been involved for the last 18 years with the North Slope Borough and the communication seems to be pretty much one way. A lot of things that were said during EISs, during scoping meetings, and during all of these other meetings are often left out. It would be interesting to see how many of the comments that our people and organizations have made actually made it into an EIS. That would show, I think, when we are trying to express our concerns, how that really is understood by the MMS or the people that are doing the EISs. I would like to see that in your study.

Michael Downs: Yes that definitely is a part of the study; going over those public testimony transcripts, looking at the scoping comments, looking at the comments on those EISs, for those themes, issues, and concerns, and seeing if they have been addressed and how have those changed over time. And how better it can be a two-way communication to effectively communicate that back to MMS.

Rex Okakok,Sr.: It would also be interesting to see during these meetings what was actually presented and what was not. So often the comments that we make in the North Slope are what was not presented or lack of information. We have been voicing these concerns for the last thirty years and we are still addressing them. So I hope that this study that you are doing will show the Federal agencies that they need to really improve communications and how they communicate. And how they take all of that information and include it in their documents not just as comments but also as something that can change the language in the EISs in all of these studies.

Bill Streever: It is good to see this kind of study. I will be interested to see how it comes out. The oil companies, at least ConocoPhillips and BP, have people whose job is to work on understanding the concerns of the native community like an external affairs liaison. Does MMS have a similar position? You had a list of study personnel but it didn't look as though there was anyone from the other culture on this list. I didn't see any Iñupiat names on the list. That seemed curious to me.

Michael Downs: On your first question, I don't know that I can respond to the position internal to MMS.

Dee Williams: We do have public affairs officers.

Bill Streever: Specifically tasked with understanding the native community?

Tom Newbury: And Albert Barros, perhaps John Goll could comment on his role.

John Goll: We do have a community liaison position similar to external affairs. But we also try to have a lot of our managers and others go directly to the communities to hear directly from the community. We do that on a number of different issues. It sounds like this study will be going into that it quite a bit to document what does happen.

Michael Downs: To your second question on the composition of the team, you are right. There are no North Slope residents on the core team. Obviously the study itself is intended to be collaborative both with the agency and the stakeholders. It is a third party study. But I would expect as in other studies that there would be at least a local liaison added to the team during the process. But at this point we do not have local residents as team members.

Rex Okakok, Sr.: I noticed that in the groups listed that are going to be working on the project, one resource that I would recommend would be the Alaska Federation of Natives (AFN). They have some good baseline studies that they have been doing for many years. University of Alaska Anchorage's Patricia Cochran would also be a good person to be involved.

Michael Downs: Thank you.

Discussion from the Barrow IUM:

George Olemaun: You said this study is just starting. According to your summary, it won't be ready until 2006. What are you expecting then?

Michael Downs: It is just starting. The first part of the study is to look at existing records, all of the testimony and input that has happened so far, beginning to contact the local institutions. But the bulk of the study will take place late this year and in to next year. So it will be the end of 2006.

George Olemaun: You will be back in the community?

Michael Downs: Yes, absolutely, several times.

Doreen Lampe: So you are going to make some effort to have these committees established in the villages? What is your intent?

Michael Downs: On the North Slope, it will be Barrow-focused.

Doreen Lampe: And the members will be from where?

Michael Downs: We will be working with local institutions. Depending upon who would like to participate, they will be drawn from a number of the same groups that we are working with for the bowhead whale study; local government, corporations, local village, as well as interested individuals.

Doreen Lampe: Will you be presenting to the village tribes?

Michael Downs: Absolutely. They will be invited to join the process.

Doreen Lampe: When would you expect to be starting?

Michael Downs: Probably the initial contacts will be in late May.

Doreen Lampe: Once this communication is opened, then what?

Michael Downs: We will have focus group meetings to talk about issues and the results of what we have found so far, in terms of obstacles to communication based on the written record. Then we will enlist help in talking about the obstacles to communication in the past, ways to improve that, and helping to design a written two-way communication to between stakeholders and the agency.

Doreen Lampe: How many times a year will you be meeting?

Michael Downs: Over the course of this study which runs to the end of 2006, we would meet about three to four times over the next year and a half.

Doreen Lampe: These are communications relating to concerns here in Barrow?

Michael Downs: Two–way communication. MMS is concerned that they are not effectively communicating the technical information that they need to communicate about their programs and technology. Part of MMS' responsibilities is to communicate to communities. MMS is also concerned that they are not hearing some of the messages from the communities in the most effective way. So it is a study to look at the process of that written communication between the agency and stakeholders.

Doreen Lampe: Once that is done, MMS will then have a more effective way of having town meetings?

Michael Downs: We will focus on written communication, newsletters, written public input, and written agency communication. It would be a supplement to the town meetings and the face-to-face meetings. This is more focused on written communication, not meetings themselves.

Doreen Lampe: On all of the studies that MMS funds?

Michael Downs: Yes.

Craig George: I would like to follow up on Doreen's questions. After having lived here awhile, it seems that if you want to get a message across, you have to use a number of different types of communication: verbal, written, one-on-one.

Also, in our experience, it seems like having someone in the community over a long period of time so that people get to know them would make a huge difference. So those kinds of things are not going to be necessarily a part of your project. This is just to figure out how to get written communication to work better?

Michael Downs: Yes. I know that MMS appreciates that communication is a multilevel process. The importance of face-to-face communication is absolutely recognized. This particular effort is focused on the written component of that, as one of many components.

SOCIAL AND ECONOMIC ASSESSMENT OF MAJOR OIL SPILL LITIGATION SETTLEMENT

John S. Petterson, Ph.D.

Impact Assessment, Inc., 2166 Avenida de la Playa, Suite F, La Jolla, CA 92037
(858) 459-0142, Email: iai@san.rr.com

This presentation describes ongoing social and economic research of major oil spill litigation and settlement processes as these bear relevance to effective management of oil and gas industry activities on the OCS. The research involves longitudinal data collection and analysis regarding Exxon Valdez oil spill (EVOS) litigation/settlement processes as these affect residents of select communities on Kodiak Island. The work is being conducted under the general hypothesis that post-spill restoration monies and litigation settlement awards will tend to amplify social, economic, and demographic trends at household, community, and regional levels of analysis.

The project is being conducted in two principal phases. Phase One involves ethnographic and archival research conducted to describe and assess relevant social, economic, and demographic conditions in the study communities prior to anticipated large-scale disbursement of litigation settlement monies. Similar research is being conducted in a Southeast Alaska "reference" community not affected by the spill or settlement processes, and a case study has been developed for a Kodiak community affected by earlier EVOS-related disbursements. Phase Two will involve description and reassessment of conditions in the study and reference communities subsequent to actual large-scale disbursement of litigation settlement monies.

Baseline description and comparative analysis relevant to the socioeconomic effects of the litigation and settlement processes for the study communities are underway and will be disseminated in a project Interim report. A final report will provide description and comparative analysis of the empirical outcome of those processes, and general recommendations for effective management of potential future oil spills and related litigation and settlement procedures in the United States.

Discussion:

Tom Newbury: My impression is that Kodiak "feels" like it was clobbered by the *Exxon Valdez* oil spill but in fact there was not that much oil. It wasn't as though the island was surrounded by oil. The third slide that you showed gave that impression.

John Petterson: What you say is correct. Some beaches had minimal impact. If we had the question we had earlier about what is the objective impact? Did they have oil on their beaches? Well to them it really didn't matter whether it actually hit their beach or it hit a subsistence area. They felt like they were impacted even if their own harbor wasn't.

ANNUAL ASSESSMENT OF SUBSISTENCE BOWHEAD WHALING NEAR CROSS ISLAND, 2004

Michael Galginaitis

Applied Sociocultural Research, 608 West 4th Avenue,
Post Office Box 101352, Anchorage AK 99510-1352
(907) 272-6811, Fax (907) 222-6023, E-mail: msgalginaitis@gci.net

The Cross Island Bowhead Whaling Documentation project (formally titled as above) began with the 2001 field season as a component of the Arctic Nearshore Impact Monitoring in Development Area (ANIMIDA) program. The ANIMIDA program, designed to monitor and measure some potential effects of the Northstar and Liberty development prospects, formally ended after the 2003 field season, but the Cross Island (and most other components) have been extended through the 2006 field season as parts of the cANIMIDA program. This presentation reports the results of the 2004 field season of the Cross Island Bowhead Whaling project. After the summary of 2004 results, discussion will focus on a brief comparison of information from 2001-2004. Little attention will be given to explicit questions of methodology and project development in this presentation, as these issues have been extensively covered in the extant Annual Reports and the Final Report prepared for the ANIMIDA project.

Four crews from Nuiqsut whaled during 2004, under the same captains as in 2003. The quota for Nuiqsut was again four whales, but only three were taken. Weather was relatively poor and conditions for whaling marginal for much of the season. The three whales taken were judged to provide enough for the village, and the 4th strike was "banked" rather than to stay on Cross Island longer in potentially worsening conditions. The number of whales observed by the whalers was not noted by the whalers as unusual and whales were found within the their "normal" migration path. One crew went out to Cross Island on August 15, much earlier than had been the case in previous years. The second crew did not go to Cross Island until August 30, and the third and fourth crews on September 4. The first day of effective scouting for whales was September 5, after all crews had reached Cross Island and weather had improved. Whales were taken on September 5, 6, and 14, at an average distance of 8.8 miles from Cross Island (preliminary). All boats left for Nuiqsut on September 17 or 18, although some did not arrive until September 19.

One crew used one boat, while the three others used two boats each (and one used a third boat during the second part of their season). Boats went out scouting for whales on 12 different days. The average trip lasted 6 hours 48 minutes, covered about 44 miles, and went about 12 miles from Cross Island. The number of crews scouting for whales on each of these days ranged from 1 to 4, and the number of boats from 1 to 7. A boat, or even a crew, whaling by itself is unusual and was due to the unusual circumstances of one crew going out to Cross Island much before the other three. This crew scouted for whales by itself on five days (using either 1 or 2 boats), primarily before the other crews went to Cross Island. After all crews had arrived at Cross Island, an average scouting effort consisted of just under 3 crews using 4.7 boats. On days when whales were taken, 3 or 4 crews were out scouting, with from 4 to 7 boats. Boat crews ranged from 2 to 8, with an average of 3.7. Of the 41 cases, a boat crew size of 3 had a frequency of 16 and a boat crew size of 4 a frequency of 15. One crew accounted for all boat crews over 5, and another for all boat crews under 3.

Discussion:

Jim Bennett: You mentioned the presence of walrus for the first time and a large number of polar bears. Is there any hypothesis as to why? Is it significant?

Michael Galginaitis: What the whalers were telling me is they assumed that the walrus were there because they drifted over on the ice. The ice conditions were different. Perhaps the ice broke up sooner than it usually does. There wasn't a whole lot of ice out there. But they did find the walrus on the floating ice. The walrus that came up on the island died of natural causes the next day. They assumed it was sick, may have been drifting, and had not been able to feed.

For the polar bears, again, they related that to the ice. The ice was so far out that was why there were so many polar bears close to the island.

Jim Bennett: As a follow up to that, were there any problems or conflicts between the polar bears and the butchering process?

Michael Galginaitis: Certainly, there was always someone on polar bear guard. Bears were hazed to keep them away from the butchering. As in previous years, there was some polar bear mortality. But people generally use what they take. If you shoot a bear, you have to take care of it.

Discussion from the Barrow IUM:

Tim Holder: How is the whale meat taken from West Dock to Nuiqsut?

Michael Galginaitis: It varies from year to year but last year it was flown on Northern Air Cargo. That has been the case more often than not in recent years. Sometimes they wait until winter and truck it to Oliktok Point, then it can be taken by boat to Nuiqsut.

Jim Bennett: You mentioned that one year they harvested three whales and that was deemed adequate for village needs. What does that mean and how was that determination made?

Michael Galginaitis: Nuiqsut has a quota of four whales. They say that the community prefers four small whales of 25 to 28 ft. That is because they are easier to butcher, they are more tender, and provide enough for themselves and to share. With three whales, if you get whales bigger than 25 ft, in this case, it was 45 ft, 33 ft, and 32 ft; a 45 ft whale is a good-sized whale. Because it is bigger around, the amount of muktuk and meat that you get increases with the square rather than directly with the increase in length. A 45 ft whale gives you much more than twice a much as a 25 ft whale. It takes longer to butcher. If you take four big whales, you are going to tire your crew especially at Cross Island where you are limited to the people on hand. So most wise whaling captains will go after smaller whales if possible. If it gets late in the season and they haven't taken any whales, they will strike any whale that they see. If it is early in the season, they will wait for a smaller whale rather go immediately for a larger one.

How they deem what is enough for the community is just based on past experience. They know what whales were taken last year and if people had enough or needed more. In the most extreme cases, some people would say they have seen a little more waste than they would like. But that varies from person to person as to what they consider waste. But it is just based on their past experience and what they have found adequate.

Craig George: In Barrow, we see the same pattern when the wind speed is down that is the time whales are caught in the fall. But in the spring, wind direction is the driving force, not so much the speed. Here, clearly the biggest whales are taken early in the season. It is like there aren't any small whales. Have you looked at years of data to see if there is the same pattern at Nuiqsut?

Michael Galginaitis: I have not looked at that carefully. So I wouldn't want to make any assumptions.

Craig George: It seems like they are taking smaller whales. I've noticed that too. So there might be selection differences over the last twenty years.

Michael Galginaitis: Yes, they explicitly say that their goal is to take smaller whales. Although, because of the weather especially the last two years, they have not been able to be as selective as they would have liked. In 2001, they couldn't have been selective because they weren't seeing many whales at all.

But I have more than enough research questions to look at with past information too. So that is certainly on the list.

A STUDY OF THE DRIFT GILLNET FISHERY AND OIL/GAS INDUSTRY INTERACTIONS AND MITIGATION POSSIBILITIES IN COOK INLET

Edward W. Glazier, Ph.D.

Impact Assessment, Inc.
2166 Avenida de la Playa, Suite F, La Jolla, CA 92037
(858) 459-0142, Email: eglazier@ec.rr.com

Drift gillnet fishery participants active in Cook Inlet deploy long nets from small boats in treacherous rip zones where salmon tend to congregate. These same grounds overlay rich oil and gas resources. As such, oil and gas industry activity potentially occurring in federal jurisdiction waters of the Inlet could lead to various challenges for both parties, including those associated with fishing and navigating around prospective drilling platforms; interaction between fishing, oil and gas, and other vessels; and oil spills or other accidents. Although drift fishery participants acknowledge regional dependence on the oil and gas industry, and platforms have been operational in the state jurisdiction waters of Cook Inlet since the mid-1970s, support for new offshore exploration or production activity is diminished by the potential for net wrapping; interaction with large freighters and tankers; and past experience with oil spills and involvement in protracted spill litigation processes.

This ITM presentation describes ethnographic research undertaken for MMS Alaska OCS Region to identify ways in which potentially challenging spatial interactions between the drift fleet and oil and gas industry activities could be mitigated, and management of fisheries and oil and gas resources appropriately balanced, should offshore development eventually occur in the region. Fishermen participating in the project have argued for specific mitigation opportunities. These include institutional arrangements that would formally empower their involvement in future fisheries and oil and gas resource management decisions, and offshore development mitigation "trade-offs" that would improve chronically poor market conditions for salmon while reducing regulatory limits on the area and length of season allowable for commercial drift fishing.

Discussion:

Lois Epstein: Did you ask any questions of the fishermen or did they offer any comments about the discharges coming from the oil and gas operations?

Ed Glazier: That was a concern that we actually brought to the table. Based on MMS EIS work there were some issues with discharges. It was superceded by this looming concern over the physical obstruction by platforms.

Lois Epstein: Did you have documentation of that in your materials?

Ed Glazier: Yes. There was another issue about there being more flow farther down on the OCS than farther north. And that would some how mitigate the problem. This is what the fishermen were saying too.

Lois Epstein: What is being done with your findings? Will it be translated into policy?

Ed Glazier: We did produce a report. Maybe Dee Williams of MMS can respond?

Dee Williams: I'll try to answer that to some degree. The agency has been involved in communicating the information to relevant stakeholder groups including agencies in the Department of Natural Resources for the State, to oil industry stakeholders. I just traveled a week ago to Kenai to present the findings to salmon fisheries stakeholder groups. The findings from the study are still being disseminated and processed. We are still scheduled to hold a lease sale in Cook Inlet in May 2006. The other significant thing to mention is that this study was timed and intended primarily to be a post-lease type of information that would go into structuring potential mitigation for prospective leasing activities. The sale that immediately followed the research was cancelled. So, in a sense, that question has been put on hold for the future. Now the ongoing lease with the Cosmopolitan Unit, of course, is also a post-lease situation. Whether or not that becomes influential in decision making about whether and when to proceed with development activities in Cosmopolitan, we don't know. That is an interesting question to observe. Does that satisfy you or can I help with some other information?

Lois Epstein: Well, I am interested in the possibility of it being used in the next lease sale. I would like to get a copy of the information.

Tim Holder: In your information packets, there is a sheet about MMS' ESPIS program where you can access all of our studies on the web. So you can just go to that and search, you will find it there.

Kate Wedemeyer: Could you contrast the perceptions of the people who are working on the drill rigs to those of the drift fishers?

Ed Glazier: Well, I can try. These are small towns. Some of the platform workers used to be fishermen and some of the fishermen have been platform workers. So there is some understanding on both sides of how things work. We asked some of the old time platform workers to tell us what they had seen. A couple of stories surfaced about net wrappings in the 1970s when drifters worked farther north in the Inlet. Some of the old time fishermen were quite vivid when they thought about some of their experiences around the platforms. If you get a net close to a platform or you have to get out of the way of a platform, it's pretty big deal - in their memory, at least. Some of their stories were quite interesting, wrapping a net, then waiting for the tide to go slack, and going back to the platform to pull the net off.

John Petterson: At one of the platforms that we visited we asked the workers about this issue of conflict, "How many times has it happened? Have you helped them out? Pulled the net? Helped get the nets out?" They remembered helping but that was something like twenty years ago. We then asked how often do they have conflicts now. They looked kind of dumbfounded. We asked when was the last time they had seen a fishing vessel near the platform. They said fifteen years. They hadn't had any interaction in so long because they changed the fishing zones to be so distance.

Steve Braund: Did you talk to any set net groups? How far offshore is that no fishing zone? There are set netters that go a mile or so off the beach.

Ed Glazier: That zone is about a mile. We talked to some set netters but didn't include any of that in the analysis given our intense focus on the drift netters.

Steve Braund: I thought I heard you say that there was no fishing north of the area that the drifters fish. There is no drift gill net fishing, but there is set net fishing.

Ed Glazier: They told us what their contemporary range was.

Steve Braund: I recall that most of those offshore rigs are north of the Forelands and there are not many south of the Forelands. It has been closed to drift gill netting north of the Forelands for decades. It would seem to me that the concern would be seeing new platforms coming into an area where drift fishers currently fish as opposed to talking about an interaction in an area where most of the platforms are north of where they fish.

Ed Glazier: Right. We sought that information because it was the only example of the net wrapping issue.

SUBSISTENCE MAPPING: NUIQSUT, KAKTOVIK, AND BARROW

Stephen R. Braund[1], Taqulik Hepa[2], John Craighead George [2], Harry Brower Jr. [2], Thomas Olemaun[2], Sharon Rudolph[3], Scot McQueen[4], Dr. Jack A. Kruse[5], and Dr. Jeffrey C. Johnson[6]

[1]Stephen R. Braund & Associates P.O. Box 1480, Anchorage, AK 99510
(907) 276-8222, Fax (907) 276-6117, E-mail: srba@alaska.net

[2]North Slope Borough Department of Wildlife Management
Box 69 Barrow, AK 99723, (907) 852-0350

[3]Encompass Data & Mapping 518 W. 19th Avenue Anchorage, AK 99503
(907) 563-8558, E-Mail: encompass@gci.net

[4]ESRI-Northwest 606 Columbia St. NW Suite 300, Olympia, WA 98501-1099
(360) 754-4727 ext. 8947, E-Mail: smcqueen@esri.com

[5]Institute of Social & Economic Research University of Alaska Anchorage
(413) 367-2240; FAX (413) 367-0092, E-mail: afjak@uaa.alaska.edu

[6]Institute for Coastal & Marine Resources and Department of Sociology East Carolina University,
Greenville, NC 27858-4353 (252) 328-1753 E-Mail: johnsonje@mail.ecu.edu

The purpose of this project is to collect subsistence information in Barrow, Nuiqsut, and Kaktovik and to develop a Geographic Information System (GIS) that describes subsistence hunting and fishing activities for selected resources. The focus is on the collection of data and description of contemporary subsistence patterns while accommodating the incorporation of past and future subsistence data to enable the analysis of changes in patterns over time. The study team has designed the GIS database, gained community approval of the project, and systematically selected a sample of active and knowledgeable harvesters in Nuiqsut and Kaktovik using social networking methods. The Barrow sampling selection is ongoing.

The study team has conducted subsistence-mapping interviews in Nuiqsut with the Kuukpikmiut Subsistence Oversight Panel, Inc. (KSOPI) assisting team members with the interviews. The interviews focus on subsistence harvests of bowhead whales, ringed seals, caribou, Arctic cisco, broad whitefish, Arctic char, eiders and geese. Mapped information being collected for the past 12 months includes resource harvest areas, travel routes, travel methods, and camps and cabins. Additional information being collected for each resource for the most recent harvest in the past 12 months includes harvest location, number of participants, duration of hunt, and harvest amount.

The results of this project will be used in Minerals Management Service's evaluation of potential effects of OCS exploration and development in the Beaufort Sea OCS region, as needed for future Environmental Assessment and Environmental Impact Statement analyses. Empirically based and methodologically documented subsistence information on the locations of subsistence activities is a necessary element in those assessments. Furthermore, an effective GIS system could facilitate monitoring of subsistence patterns over time and assist in identifying mitigation measures.

Discussion:

John Petterson: We or actually Michael Galginaitis did subsistence mapping for Nuiqsut in 1990 and 1991. I recall that the maps were much broader. We didn't use this methodology of last year. You are now mapping the effect of technology and age shifts over time. The people that you are interviewing now are probably younger than the people that we interviewed. A larger percentage of the population might have been involved in subsistence a decade ago, etc. Okay, that is a conceptual issue. You have approached it in a methodological way that seems quite sound. But the conceptual issue may be the bigger problem because you are going to have maps that are constrained. You are going to have caribou maps that show essentially access routes for three-wheelers or snow machines. Technology is going to influence this. And, over time, it will leave the impression that these other areas are not subsistence use areas when in fact, at least conceptually to the people that live there, they still are. But they may not have been used in the last year, two years, or even three years. That doesn't matter in their minds. It is still their subsistence area. It may lead someone else to conclude otherwise.

Steve Braund: Good point. The map I showed was done 18 months ago. The area that we identified as subsistence use is called "contemporary subsistence use." On the map, we indicated use areas as per Sverre Pedersen's ADF&G 1979 lifetime use areas. So with every map, you need to include that lifetime use area. And that is what we have done as a policy. We always try to put the 1979 lifetime area and the contemporary area that I have defined as the last ten years. No one has complained about that period being used to define "contemporary" in communities. We are calling current or contemporary the last ten years. We have documented that period for Nuiqsut. We have part of that use documented for Kaktovik. I think it is pretty well documented in Barrow. It wouldn't behoove anyone to go back out and redo that. I think your point is very well taken. I think that you always have to show both [the broad use area as well as last year] on every map.

Discussion from the Barrow IUM:

Craig George: Why don't hunting areas and dots that look like they represent harvest locations match?

Steve Braund: So you arer asking why don't we have a hunting area over a dot? This is a draft work in progress. We have to edit and refine it.

Craig George: So you didn't define the caribou hunting areas based on the harvest locations?

Steve Braund: No. We asked respondents "Where did you hunt?" But you are right the map should have at least shown that the hunter went [hunted] there if we put a dot [harvest] there or so you would have thought. This might be as simple, these are in the river, and so it might be as simple as a little glitch in the coding.

There are two different questions we asked respondents. "Where did you hunt caribou last year?" These maps show the cumulative polygons and there were only 14 interviews. Another question we asked later was, "During the last hunt of caribou in the last year, where did you harvest a caribou?" And that is where the dots are on the map.

Dave Rugh: I appreciate some of the concerns here. This is good documentation. I am very impressed with how you are doing this. But what is the next step as far as OCS development? Another way of putting this question: what if 25 years ago you went forward and no one in the community asked any questions. No one came forward. How different would the scene be now than what it is?

Steve Braund: I agree with you. We do have data from 25 years ago. Coming to these meetings, participating in the studies, you start to produce products. There is a major port expansion that they want to put out at Red Dog mine, and they are waiting to see some of the results of that study. I think by coming, by continually making your point [you can accomplish something]. I agree with what the gentleman from MMS who said, "Don't stop." There is another five-year lease plan coming. If you don't come and if they hadn't done this study, it could be worse. I don't know if I have answered your question or not.

These data [on the map] are just for caribou. We haven't done the offshore analysis of this. They are looking for disposal sites for dredging. Mind you we are totally objective. We are just gathering information, trying to compile the information, and put it in a format that addresses both the local concerns and the agencies concerns, and then try to put the two together. It is not our job to interpret what to do then or how to mitigate. That is between the stakeholders and the developers and the agencies.

Attachment I - Agendas

Minerals Management Service (MMS) – Alaska Outer Continental Shelf (OCS) Region
10th Information Transfer Meeting (ITM): March 14-16, 2005
Anchorage Marriott Downtown, Anchorage, Alaska

Final Agenda

For another meeting related to the ITM see the last page of this agenda.

Monday, March 14, 2005

7:30 am Registration

MMS Introduction

7:50 am Welcome to the ITM and the Alaska Environmental Studies Program
Cleve Cowles, Ph.D., Chief Environmental Studies Section, MMS, Alaska OCS Region

Alaska OCS Region Activities and Environmental Assessment Process
Mr. Paul Stang, Regional Supervisor for Leasing and Environment, MMS, Alaska OCS Region

Physical Oceanography

8:20 am Integration of Physical Oceanography Studies
Richard Prentki, Ph.D., MMS

MMS Session Chair: Ms. Kate Wedemeyer

8:30 am Water and Ice Dynamics of Cook Inlet
Mark Johnson, Ph.D., Institute of Marine Sciences (IMS), University of Alaska Fairbanks UAF)

9:00 am Observations of Hydrography in Central Cook Inlet, Alaska, during Diurnal and Semidiurnal Tidal Cycles and
Physical Measurements and Seasonal Boundary Conditions in Cook Inlet, Alaska
Steve Okkonen, Ph.D., IMS, UAF

9:30 am High-Resolution Numerical Modeling of Near-Surface Weather Conditions over Alaska'sCook Inlet and Shelikof Strait
Peter Olsson, Ph.D., University of Alaska Anchorage

10:00 am Break

10:15 am Sea Ice Modeling for Beaufort and Chukchi Seas (FRAM)
Matt Pruis, Ph.D., NorthWest Research Associates, Bellevue, Washington

10:45 am Sea-Ice-Ocean-Oil Spill Modeling System for the Nearshore Beaufort and Chukchi Seas: Improvements and Parameterization
Jia Wang, Ph.D., International Arctic Research Center, UAF

11:15 am Simulation of Landfast Sea Ice along the Alaskan Coast
Mark Hopkins, Ph.D., Cold Regions Research Environmental Laboratory, U.S. Army Corps of Engineers, Hanover, New Hampshire

11:45 am Lunch

12:50 pm Integration of Fate and Effects Studies
Richard Prentki, Ph.D., MMS

**1:00 pm Development and Testing of an Ocean Model with Wetting and Drying
Capability for Tidal Areas [Cook Inlet]**
Leo Oey, Ph.D., AOS Program, Princeton University, Princeton, New Jersey

**1:30 pm Mapping and Characterization of Recurring Spring Leads and Landfast Ice in the
Beaufort and Chukchi Seas**
Mr. Hajo Eicken, Geophysical Institute, UAF

**2:00 pm Surface Circulation Radar Mapping in Alaskan Coastal Waters: Field Study Beaufort Sea
and Cook Inlet**
Dave Musgrave, Ph.D., School of Fisheries and Ocean Sciences (SFOS), UAF
To be presented by Mr. Hank Statscewich.

Fate and Effects

MMS Session Chair: Richard Prentki, Ph.D.

Continuation of Arctic Nearshore Impact Monitoring in Development Area (cANIMIDA)

2:30 pm 1. cANIMIDA: Overview
Mr. Greg Durell, Battelle, Duxbury, Massachusetts

2:45 pm 2. Hydrocarbon Chemistry of Sediments in the Nearshore Beaufort Sea
Mr. John Brown, Exponent, Maynard, Massachusetts

3:15 pm Break

**3:30 pm 3. Sources, Concentrations, and Dispersion Pathways for Suspended Sediment and
4. Partitioning of Potential Pollutants between Dissolved and Particulate Phases**
John Trefry, Ph.D., Florida Institute of Technology, Melbourne, Florida

**4:00 pm 5. Integrated Biomonitoring and Bioaccumulation of Anthropogenic Compounds in
Biota**
Jerry Neff, Ph.D., Battelle, Duxbury, Massachusetts

**4:30 pm 6. Long Term Monitoring of the Kelp Community in the Stefansson Sound the Boulder
Patch: Detection of Change Related to Oil and Gas Development**
Ken Dunton, Ph.D., Marine Science Institute, University of Texas at Austin, Port Aransas,
Texas

7. Annual Assessment of Subsistence BowheadWhaling near Cross Island, 2004
(see Social Science and Economics, Wednesday March 16)

5:00 pm Adjourn

Tuesday, March 15, 2005

Fate and Effects *(continued)*

MMS Session Chair: Mr. Richard Newman

8:00 am Persistence of Crude Oil Spills on Open Water
Ian Buist, P. Eng., S.L. Ross Environmental Research Ltd., Ottawa, Ontario, Canada

8:30 am **Improvements in the Fault Tree Approach to Oil Spill Occurrence Estimators for the Beaufort Sea**
Frank G. Bercha, Ph.D., Bercha Group, Calgary, Alberta, Canada

9:00 am **Empirical Weathering Properties of Oil in Snow and Ice**
Ian Buist, P. Eng., S.L. Ross Environmental Research Ltd., Ottawa, Ontario, Canada

Biology

MMS Session Chair: Jeff Gleason, Ph.D.

9:30 am **Large-Scale Movements and Habitat Characteristics of King Eiders throughout the Nonbreeding Period**
Ms. Laura Phillips, Institute of Arctic Biology, UAF

10:00 am Break

10:05 am Integration of Biology Studies
Jeff Gleason, Ph.D., MMS and Ms. Kate Wedemeyer, MMS

10:15 am Susceptibility of Sea Ice Biota to Disturbances in the Shallow Beaufort Sea. Phase I: Biological Coupling of Sea Ice with Pelagic and Benthic Realms
Bodil Bluhm, Ph.D., SFOS, IMS, UAF

10:45 am Foraging Ecology of Common Ravens (*Corvus corax*) on Alaska's Coastal Plain and its Relationship to Oil and Gas Development
Ms. Stacia Backensto, Institute of Arctic Biology, UAF

MMS Session Chair: Ms. Kate Wedemeyer

11:15 am Analysis of Variation in Abundance of Arctic Cisco in the Colville River: Analysis of Patterns in Existing Data
Franz Mueter, Ph.D., Sigma Plus Statistical Computing, Fairbanks, Alaska

11:45 am Lunch

1:00 pm **Locating Overwintering Fish Habitat: Sagavanirktok and Colville Rivers/Beaufort Sea**
Mr. Claude Duguay, Geophysical Institute, UAF

1:30 pm **Coastal Marine Institute (CMI)—University of Alaska Fairbanks Overview of CMI & MMS and Synopsis of 2 Recently Approved CMI studies**
Vera Alexander, Ph.D., Coastal Marine Institute/IMS/UAF

2:00 pm **Ongoing Projects of the Department of Wildlife Management, North Slope Borough**
Robert Suydam, Ph.D. and Mr. Craig George, Department of Wildlife Management, North Slope Borough

2:30 pm **Break**

2:35 pm **Integration of Protected Species Studies**
Charles Monnett, Ph.D., MMS

Protected Species

MMS Session Chair: Charles Monnett, Ph.D.

2:45 pm **Demography and Behavior of Polar Bears Feeding on Stranded Marine Mammal Carcasses**
Ms. Susanne Miller, Marine Mammal Management, U. S. Fish and Wildlife Service (USFWS)

3:15 pm **Polar Bear Population Monitoring Workshop**
Mr. Craig Perham, Marine Mammal Management, USFWS

3:45 pm **Status of King and Common Eiders Migrating Past Point Barrow, Alaska**
Robert Suydam, Ph.D., DWM, NSB, Barrow.

4:15 pm **Population Structure of Common Eider Nesting on Coastal Barrier Islands Adjacent to Oil Facilities in the Beaufort Sea**
Kevin McCracken, Ph.D., Institute of Arctic Biology, UAF
To be presented by Ms. Sarah Sonsthagen.

4:45 pm **Breeding Biology and Habitat Use of King Eiders on the Coastal Plain of Northern Alaska**
Ms. Rebecca McGuire, Institute of Arctic Biology, UAF

5:15 pm **Adjourn**

Wednesday, March 16, 2005

Protected Species *(continued)*

MMS Session Chair: Jeff Gleason, Ph.D.

8:00 am **Protocol to Deflect Migrating Bowhead Whales Away from an Oil Spill**
W. John Richardson, Ph.D., LGL Limited, King City, Ontario, Canada

8:30 am **Analysis of Covariance of Human Activities and Sea Ice in Relation to Fall Migrations of Bowhead Whales**
W. John Richardson, Ph.D., LGL Limited, King City, Ontario, Canada

9:00 am **Distribution and Abundance of Harbor Seals in the Cook Inlet: Seasonal Variability in Relation to Key Life History Events**
Peter Boveng, Ph.D., National Marine Mammal Laboratory, (NMML) Alaska Fisheries Science Center (AFSC), Seattle, Washington

9:30 am **Break**

MMS Session Chair: Mr. Richard Newman

9:45 am **Seasonal Distribution of Steller's Eiders in Cook Inlet, Alaska**
Mr. William Larned, Office of Migratory Bird Management, USFWS

10:15 am **Movements and Habitat Use of Harbor Seals in Cook Inlet**
Peter Boveng, Ph.D., NMML, AFSC, Seattle, Washington

10:45 am **Aerial Photography of Bowhead Whales to Estimate the Size of the Bering-Chukchi-Beaufort Population**
David Rugh, NMML, AFSC, Seattle, Washington

Social Science and Economics

MMS Session Chair: Dee Williams, Ph.D.

11:15 am Quantitative Description of Potential Impacts of OCS Activities on Bowhead Whale Hunting and Subsistence Activities in the Beaufort Sea
Michael Downs, Ph.D., EDAW, Inc., San Diego, California

11:45 am Lunch

12:50 pm Integration of Social Science Studies
Dee Williams, Ph.D., MMS

1:00 pm North Slope Economy, 1965 to Present
Leah Cuyno, Ph.D., Northern Economics, Inc., Anchorage, Alaska

1:30 pm Researching Technical Dialogue with Alaskan Coastal Communities: Analysis of the Social, Cultural, Linguistic, and Institutional Parameters of Public/Agency Communication Patterns
Michael Downs, Ph.D., EDAW, Inc., San Diego, California

MMS Session Chair: Mr. Tim Holder

2:00 pm Social and Economic Assessment of Major Oil Spill Litigation Settlement
John Petterson, Ph.D., Impact Assessment, Inc., La Jolla, California

2:30 pm Annual Assessment of Subsistence Bowhead Whaling near Cross Island, 2004
Mr. Michael Galginaitis, Applied Sociocultural Research, Anchorage, Alaska

3:00 pm Break

3:10 pm Integration of Economics Studies
Mr. Tim Holder, MMS

3:15 pm A Study of the Drift Gillnet Fishery and Oil/Gas Industry Interactions and Mitigation Possibilities in Cook Inlet
Ed Glazier, Ph.D., Impact Assessment, Inc., La Jolla, California

3:45 pm Subsistence Mapping at Nuiqsut, Kaktovik, and Barrow
Mr. Stephen R. Braund, Stephen R. Braund and Associates, Anchorage, Alaska

4:15 pm Adjourn

Other meeting related to the ITM

Monday, March 14, 5:15 pm: Anchorage Marriott Downtown - same room as ITM
Meeting to Discuss Coordinating Ongoing and Proposed Studies: Physical Oceanography, Modeling of Sea Ice and Circulation in the Beaufort Sea, Chukchi Sea, and Cook Inlet
Ronald Lai, Ph.D., MMS, Meeting Leader.

5

Minerals Management Service
Alaska Outer Continental Shelf Region
Information Update Meeting in Barrow, Alaska
FINAL AGENDA – Friday March 18, 2005

8:00 am   **Registration**

8:15 am   **Meeting Introduction/Meeting Purpose**
Cleve Cowles, Ph.D., Chief, Environmental Studies Section, MMS, Alaska OCS Region, Anchorage, Alaska

8:30 am   **Ongoing Projects of the Department of Wildlife Management, North Slope Borough**
Mr. Craig George Department of Wildlife Management, (DWM) North Slope Borough (NSB) Barrow, Alaska

9:00 am   **cANIMIDA – continuation of Arctic Nearshore Impact Monitoring in Development Area**
Richard Prentki, Ph.D., MMS, Alaska OCS Region, Anchorage, Alaska

9:30 am   **Analysis of Variation in Abundance of Arctic Cisco in the Colville River**
Mr. Stephen R. Braund, Stephen R. Braund and Associates, Anchorage, Alaska

10:00 am   **Break**

10:15 am   **Locating Overwintering Fish Habitat: Sagavanirktok, Colville Rivers/Beaufort Sea**
Mr. Claude Duguay, University of Alaska Fairbanks, Fairbanks, Alaska

10:45 am   **Aerial Photography of Bowhead Whales to Estimate the Size of the Bering-Chukchi-Beaufort Population**
Mr. David Rugh, National Marine Mammal Laboratory, Seattle, Washington

11:15 am   **Status of King and Common Eiders Migrating Past Point Barrow, Alaska**
Robert Suydam, Ph.D., DWM, NSB, Barrow, Alaska

11:45 am   **Lunch**

1:15 pm   **Researching Technical Dialogue with Alaskan Coastal Communities: Analysis of the Social, Cultural, Linguistic, and Institutional Parameters of Public/Agency Communication Patterns**
Michael Downs, Ph.D., EDAW, Inc, San Diego, California

1:45 pm   **North Slope Economy, 1965 to Present**
Leah Cuyno, Ph.D., Northern Economics, Inc., Anchorage, Alaska

2:15 pm   **Annual Assessment of Subsistence Bowhead Whaling Near Cross Island, 2004**
Mr. Michael Galginaitis, Applied Sociocultural Research, Anchorage, Alaska

2:45 pm   **Break**

3:00 pm   **Quantitative Description of Potential Impacts of OCS Activities on Bowhead Whale Hunting and Subsistence Activities in the Beaufort Sea**
Michael Downs, Ph.D., EDAW, Inc, San Diego, California

3:30 pm   **Subsistence Mapping at Nuiqsut, Kaktovik, and Barrow**
Mr. Stephen R. Braund, Stephen R. Braund & Associates, Anchorage, Alaska

4:00 pm   **General Question and Answer Period**

5:00 pm   **End of Meeting**

Attachment II – Attendee Lists

* = Speaker

Ahlfeld, Tom
Minerals Management Service
381 Elden Street
Herndon, VA 20170-4817
(703) 787-1711, FAX (703) 787-1053
thomas.ahlfeld@mms.gov

Alexander, Vera*
Director
Coastal Marine Institute
University of Alaska Fairbanks
Fairbanks, AK 99775
(907) 474-6824
vera@sfos.uaf.edu

Backensto, Stacia*
Institute of Arctic Biology
University of Alaska Fairbanks
P.O. Box 757000
Fairbanks, AK 99775-7000
(907) 474-5505, FAX (907) 474-6716
ftsab@uaf.edu

Bailey, Alan
Petroleum News
(907) 345-9622
abailey@petroluemnews.com

Beesley, Anne
Oasis Environmental
807 G Street
Anchorage, AK 99501
(907) 258-4880

Belli, Julia
Weston Solutions, Inc. for Unocal
909 West 9th Avenue
Anchorage, AK 99516
(907) 263-7831
bellij@unocal.com

Benner, Colleen
MMS/HQ
381 Elden Street
Herndon, VA 22170
(703) 787-1710, FAX (703) 787-1053
lee.benner@mms.gov

Bennett, James F.
Minerals Management Service
381 Elden Street
Herndon, VA 20170
(703) 787-1660, FAX (703) 787-1026
jfbennett@mms.gov

Bercha, Frank G.*
Bercha International
2926 Parkdale Blvd., N.W.
Calgary, Alberta, CANADA T2N 3S9
(403) 270-2221, FAX (403) 270-2014
berchaf@berchagroup.com

Blees, Megan
LGL Alaska Research
1101 East 76th, Suite B
Anchorage, AK 99518
(907) 562-3339, (907) 562-7223
mblees@lgl.com

Bluhm, Bodil*
IMS/SFOS
University of Alaska Fairbanks
245 O'Neill Bldg., P.O. Box 757220
Fairbanks, AK 99775-7220
(907) 474-6332, FAX (907) 474-7204
bluhm@ims.uaf.edu

Bodziak, Robert
ConocoPhillips Alaska
700 G Street
Anchorage, AK 00516
(907) 265-1495
robert.m.bodziak@conocophillips.com

Boisvert, Jennifer
ABR Inc.
P.O. Box 240268
Anchorage, AK 99508
(907) 344-6777
jboisvert@abrinc.com

Boveng, Peter*
National Marine Mammal Laboratory
Alaska Fisheries Science Center
7600 Sand Point Way, NE, Bldg. 4
Seattle, WA 98115-6349
(206) 526-4244, FAX (206) 526-6615
peter.boveng@noaa.gov

Braund, Stephen R.*
Stephen R. Braund and Associates
P.O. Box 1480
Anchorage, AK 99510
(907) 276-8222, FAX (907) 276-6117
srba@alaska.net

Bronson, Mike
BP Exploration (Alaska) Inc.
900 E. Benson Blvd.
Anchorage, AK 99519
(907) 564-4566, FAX (907) 564-5180
bronsomt@bp.com

Brown, John*
Exponent
2 Clock Tower Place, Suite 340
Maynard, MA 01754-2595
(978) 461-1221, FAX (978) 461-1223
jsbrown@exponent.com

Buist, Ian *
S.L. Ross Environmental Research, Ltd.
200-717 Belfast Rd.
Ottawa, Ontario, CANADA K1G 0Z4
(613) 232-1564, FAX (613) 232-6660
ian@slross.com

Burwell, Michael
Alaska OCS Region
Minerals Management Service
3801 Centerpoint Drive, Suite 500
Anchorage, AK 99508
(907) 334-5249

Busse, Kim
URS Corp.
2700 Gambell Street, Suite 200
Anchorage, AK 99503
(907) 261-9745
kim_busse@urscorp.com

Castellini, Michael
MMS Scientific Advisory Committee
Institute of Marine Sciences
School of Fisheries and Ocean Sciences
University of Alaska Fairbanks
Fairbanks, AK 99775
(907) 474-6825, FAX (907) 474-7204
mikec@ims.uaf.edu

Cheng, Ralph T.
U.S. Geological Survey
345 Middlefield Road
Menlo Park, CA
(650) 329-4500, FAX (650) 329-4327
rtcheng@usgs.gov

Childs, Jeff
Alaska OCS Region
Minerals Management Service
3801 Centerpoint Drive, Suite 500
Anchorage, AK 99508
(907) 334-5262 FAX (907) 334-5242
jeff.childs@mms.gov

Cologgi, John
ConocoPhillips Alaska, Inc.
700 G Street
Anchorage, AK 99577
(907) 265-6478, FAX (907) 263-4035

Colonell, Jack
URS Corporation
2700 Gambell Street, Suite 200
Anchorage, AK 99503
(907) 261-9731, FAX (907) 562-1297
jack_colonel@urscorp.com

Cowles,Cleve*, Chief
Environmental Studies Section
Alaska OCS Region
Minerals Management Service
3801 Centerpoint Drive, Suite 500
Anchorage, AK 99508
(907) 334-5281

Cuyno, Leah *
Northern Economics, Inc.
880 H Street, Suite 210
Anchorage, AK 99501
(907) 274-5600, FAX (907) 274-5601
Leah.Cuyno@norecon.com

Dasher, Douglas H.
Dept. of Environmental Conservation
State of Alaska
610 University Ave.
Fairbanks, AK 99709
(907) 451-2172, FAX (907) 451-2187
doug_dasher@dec.state.ak.us

Davis, Wendy
ABR Inc.
4141 B Street
Anchorage, AK 99508
(907) 344-6777
wdavis@abrinc.com

DeGeorge, Lynn
ConocoPhillips Alaska, Inc.
700 G Street, ATO 1932
Anchorage, AK 99510
(907) 263-4671
lynn.a.degeorge@conocophillips.com

Downs, Mike*
EDAW, Inc.
1420 Kettner Blvd., Suite 620
San Diego, CA 92101
(619) 233-1454, FAX (619) 233-0952
downsm@edaw.com

Ducher, James
BLM
222 West 7th Ave.
Anchorage, AK 99513
(907) 271-3130
jim_ducher@blm.gov

Duguay, Claude*
Geophysical Institute
University of Alaska Fairbanks
Fairbanks, AK 99775
(907) 474-6832
claude.duguay@gi.alaska.edu

Dunton, Ken *
Marine Science Institute
University of Texas at Austin
750 Channel View Drive
Port Aransas, TX 78373
(361) 749-6744, FAX (361) 749-6777
dunton@utmsi.utexas.edu

Durell, Greg *
Battelle
397 Washington Street
Duxbury, MA 02332
(781) 952-5233, FAX (781) 934-2124
durell@battelle.org

Duvall, Terra
ITM Assistant
MBC *Applied Environmental Sciences*
3000 Redhill Ave.
Costa Mesa, CA 92626
(714) 850-4830, FAX (714) 850-4840
tduvall@mbcnet.net

Easton, John
DNR
550 West 7th Ave.
Anchorage, AK 99501
(907) 269-8815
john_easton@dnristate.ak.us

Eicken, Hajo *
Geophysical Institute
University of Alaska Fairbanks
903 Koyukuk Drive, P.O. Box 757320
Fairbanks, AK 99775-7320
(907) 474-7280, FAX (907) 474-7290
hajo.eicken@gi.alaska.edu

Epstein, Lois
Cook Inlet Keeper
308 G Street, Suite 219
Anchorage, AK 99501
(907) 929-9371, FAX (907) 929-1562
lois@inletkeeper.org

Eschenbach, Ted
TGE Consulting
4376 Rendezvous Circle
AK, 99504
(907) 333-7817
ted1@alaska.net

Ezer, Tal
Princeton University
Sayre Hall, Forrestal Campus
Princeton, NJ 08544-0710
(609) 258-1318
ezer@princeton.edu

Funk, Dale
Alaska Research Associates
1101 East 26th Ave., Suite B
Anchorage, AK 99518
(907) 562-3339, FAX (907) 562-7223
dfunk@lgl.com

Galginaitis, Michael*
Applied Sociocultural Research
P.O. Box 101352
Anchorage, AK 99510-1352
(907) 272-6811, FAX (907) 222-6023
msgalginaitis@gci.net

Gardner, Lee Ann
RWJ Consulting
P.O. Box 672302
Chugiak, AK 99567
(907) 688-1400, FAX (907) 688-1400
rwjconsulting@ak.net

Gaylord, Allison
NUNA Technologies
P.O. Box 1483
Homer, AK 99603
(907) 235-3476
nunatech@usa.net

Glazier, Ed *
Impact Assessment, Inc.
2166 Avenida de la Playa, Suite F
La Jolla, CA 92037
(910) 256-2059
iai@san.rr.com

Goll, John
Regional Director
Alaska OCS Region
Minerals Management Service
3801 Centerpoint Drive, Suite 500
Anchorage, AK 99508
(907) 334-5200

Gleason, Jeffrey
Alaska OCS Region
Minerals Management Service
3801 Centerpoint Drive, Suite 500
Anchorage, AK 99508
(907) 334-5286

Greene, Ben
Alaska DNR/OPMP/ACMP/JPO
411 West 4th
Anchorage, AK 99501
(907) 257-7351
bgreene@jpo.doi.gov

Griffin, Harrison
Bureau of Land Management
6881 Abbott Loop Road
Anchorage, AK 99507
(907) 267-1446, FAX (907) 267-1304
hgriffin@ak.blm.gov

Hansen, Don
Alaska OCS Region
Minerals Management Service
3801 Centerpoint Drive, Suite 500
Anchorage, AK 99508
(907) 334-5264

Hardin, John
Battelle
703 Palomar Airport Road, Suite 350
Carlsbad, CA 92009
(760) 476-1415, FAX (760) 476-1416
hardinj@battelle.org

Havelock, Brian
ADNR/DO&G
550 W. 7th Avenue, #800
Anchorage, AK 99501
(907) 269-8807
beh@dnr.state.ak.us

Holder, Tim
ITM Coordinator
Alaska OCS Region
Minerals Management Service
3801 Centerpoint Drive, Suite 500
Anchorage, AK 99508
(907) 334-5279
Tim.Holder@mms.gov

Hopkins, Mark*
ERDC-CRREL
72 Lyme Road
Hanover, NH 03755
(603) 646-4249
Mark.A.Hopkins@erdc.usace.army.mil

Horowitz, Warren
Alaska OCS Region
Minerals Management Service
3801 Centerpoint Drive, Suite 500
Anchorage, AK 99508
(907) 334-5285

Hu, Haoguo
IARC UAF
930 Koyukuk Drive
Fairbanks, AK 99775
(907) 474-7059
hhu@iarc.uaf.edu

Isaacs, Marnie
ConocoPhillips Alaska, Inc.
700 G Street, ATO 1926
Anchorage, AK 99510
(907) 263-4576
marnie.h.isaacs@conocophillips.com

Jen, Mark
US EPA Region 10
222 W. 7th Street, #19
Anchorage, AK 99513
(907) 271-3411, FAX (907) 271-3424
jen.mark@epa.gov

Jin, Meibing
IARC/UAF
P.O. Box 757340
Fairbanks, AK 99775
(907) 474-2442
ffjm@uaf.edu

Johnson, Mark *
School of Fisheries and Ocean Sciences
University of Alaska Fairbanks
P.O. Box 757220
Fairbanks, AK 99775
(907) 474-6933
johnson@ims.uaf.edu

Johnson, Walter
Minerals Management Service
381 Elden Street
Herndon, VA 20170-4817

Kay, Quyen
ConocoPhillips Alaska, Inc.
700 G Street
Anchorage, AK 99501
(907) 265-6362
quyen.c.kay@conocophillips.com

Kruse, Kim
Dept. of Natural Resources
State of Alaska
550 W. 7th Avenue, Suite 1660
Anchorage, AK 99501
(907) 269-7473, FAX (907) 269-3981
Kim_Kruse@dnr.state.ak.us

Ji, Jeff
Minerals Management Service
381 Elden Street
Herndon, VA 20170-4817

Lai, Ronald J.
Branch of Environmental Services
Minerals Management Services
381 Elden Street,
Herndon, VA 20170-4817
(703) 787-1714, FAX (703) 787-1053
ronald.lai@mms.gov

Lanctot, Richard
USFWS
1011 East Tudor Road
Anchorage, AK 99503
(907) 786-3609, FAX (907) 786-3641
richard_lanctot@fws.gov

Larned, William*
Office of Migratory Bird Mgmt.
U.S. Fish and Wildlife Service
1011 E. Tudor Road
Anchorage, AK 99503
(907) 260-0124, FAX (907) 262-7145
William_Larned@fws.gov

Lohman, Tom
North Slope Borough
4011 Winchester Loop
Anchorage, AK 99507
(907) 349-2606, FAX (907) 349-2602
tomlohman2@aol.com

Macdonald, Colin
Northern Environmental Consulting
24 Dufferin Ave.
Pinawa, MB R0E 1L0 Canada
(204) 743-2078, FAX (204) 753-2298
northern@granite.mb.ca

Mahoney, Andy
Geophysical Institute
University of Alaska Fairbanks
Fairbanks, AK 99775
(907) 474-1156, FAX (907) 474-7290
mahoney@gi.alaska.edu

Major, Mark
ConocoPhillips Alaska, Inc.
P.O. Box 100360
Anchorage, AK 99510
(907) 265-6136, FAX (907) 265-1608
Mark.A.Major@conocophillips.com

Marcy, Suzanne
National Park Service
240 W. 5th Avenue
Anchorage, AK 99501
(907) 622-2610
suzanne_marcy@partner.nps.gov

Markowitz, Tim
LGL Alaska Research Associates
1101 East 76th, Suite B
Anchorage, AK 99518
(907) 644-2731
tmarrkowitz@lgl.com

Massey, Justin
Trustees for Alaska
1026 West 4th Ave., Suite 201
Anchorage, AK 99501
(907) 276-4244 x114, FAX (907) 276-7110
jmassey@trustees.org

Mayers, Tim
Kinnetic Laboratories Inc.
403 West 8th Ave.
Anchorage, AK 99501
(907) 276-6178, FAX (907) 278-6881
tmayers@kinneticlabs.com

McCammon, Molly
Alaska Ocean Observing System
1007 West Third Street, Suite 100
Anchorage, AK 99501
(907) 644-6703, FAX (907) 644-6780
mccammon@aoos.org

McCutcheon, Jerry
SCI
Anchorage, AK
(907) 277-3076
susitnahydronow@yahoo.com

McGuire, Rebecca*
Institute of Arctic Biology
University of Alaska Fairbanks
P.O. Box 757000
Fairbanks, AK 99775-7000
(907) 474-5505, FAX (907) 474-6716
ftrlm@uaf.edu

Miller, Susanne*
Marine Mammal Management
U.S. Fish and Wildlife Service
1011 E. Tudor Road
Anchorage, AK 99503
(907) 786-3828, FAX (907) 786-3816
susanne_miller@fws.gov

Mitchell, Chuck
President
MBC *Applied Environmental Sciences*
3000 Redhill Ave.
Costa Mesa, CA 92626
(714) 850-4830, FAX (714) 850-4840
cmitchell@mbcnet.net

Mitchell, Kathy
ITM Coordinator
MBC *Applied Environmental Sciences*
3000 Redhill Ave.
Costa Mesa, CA 92626
(714) 850-4830, FAX (714) 850-4840
kmitchell@mbcnet.net

Monnett, Charles
Alaska OCS Region
Minerals Management Service
3801 Centerpoint Drive, Suite 500
Anchorage, AK 99508
(907) 334-5282

Morse, Robert
ConocoPhillips
700 G Street
Anchorage, AK 99516
(907) 263-4112
r.k.morse@conocophillips.com

Mueter, Franz*
Sigma Plus Statistical Computing
697 Fordham Drive
Fairbanks, AK 99709
(907) 479-8815 and FAX
fmueter@alaska.net
franz.mueter@noaa.gov

Mundy, Nancy
Northern Economics, Inc
880 H Street, Suite 210
Anchorage, AK 99501
(907) 274-5600, FAX (907) 274-5601
nancy.mundy@norecon.com

Nebesky, William
DNR
505 West 7th Ave.
Anchorage, AK 99516
(907) 269-8799

Neff, Jerry*
Battelle Memorial Institute
397 Washington Street
Duxbury, MA 02332
(781) 952-5229, FAX (781) 934-2124
neffjm@battelle.org

Newbury, Tom
Alaska OCS Region
Minerals Management Service
3801 Centerpoint Drive, Suite 500
Anchorage, AK 99508
(907) 334-5263

Newman, Richard
Alaska OCS Region
Minerals Management Service
3801 Centerpoint Drive, Suite 500
Anchorage, AK 99508
(907) 334-5284

Oey, Lie-Yauw*
AOS Program, Princeton University
Sayre Hall, Forrestal Campus
Princeton, NJ 08544-0710
(609) 258-5971, FAX (609) 258-2850
lyo@aos.princeton.edu

Okakok, Sr., Rex A.
North Slope Borough
P.O. Box 69
Barrow, AK 99723\
(907) 852-0320, FAX (907) 852-0322
rex.okakok@north-slope.org

Olsson, Peter*
University of Alaska Anchorage
3200 Providence drive
Anchorage, AK
(907) 264-7449, FAX (907) 264-7444
olsson@at.uaa.alaska.edu

Paquette, Carol
ITM Assistant
MBC Applied Environmental Sciences
3000 Redhill Ave.
Costa Mesa, CA 92626
(714) 850-4830, FAX (714) 850-4840
cpaquette@mbcnet.net

Parker, Walter B.
Parker Associates, Inc.
3224 Campbell Airstrip Road
Anchorage, AK 99504
(907) 333-5189, FAX (907) 333-5153
wbparker@gci.net

Perham, Craig*
Marine Mammal Management
U.S. Fish and Wildlife Service
1011 E. Tudor Road
Anchorage, AK 99503
(907) 786-3810, FAX (907) 786-3816
craig_perham@fws.gov

Petterson, John*
Impact Assessment, Inc.
2166 Avenida de la Playa, Suite F
La Jolla, CA 92037
(858) 459-0142
iai@san.rr.com

Phillips, Laura*
Institute of Arctic Biology
University of Alaska Fairbanks
P.O. Box 757000
Fairbanks, AK 99775-7000
(907) 474-7144, FAX (907) 474-7872
fslmp@uaf.edu

Pindell, Darla
BLM
6881 Abbott Loop Road
Anchorage, AK 99507
(907) 267-1462
dpindell@blm.gov

Pokiak, Frank
Inuvialuit Game Council
Box 2120
Inuvik, NT, X0E 0T0 CANADA
(867) 777-2828, FAX (867) 777-2610
igc-js@jointsec.nt.ca

Pollock, George
Michael J. Baker, Inc.
4601 Business Park Blvd., Suite 42
Anchorage, AK 99503
(907) 273-1640, FAX (07) 351-8286
gpollock@mbakercorp.com

Prentki, Dick
Alaska OCS Region
Minerals Management Service
3801 Centerpoint Drive, Suite 500
Anchorage, AK 99508
(907) 334-5277

Presley, Bob
Texas A&M
10995 Woodlands Drive
College State, TX 77845
(979) 764-3928
bpresley@ocean.tamu.edu

Richardson, W. John*
LGL Ltd. environmental research associates
22 Fisher Street, P.O. Box 280
King City, Ontario, CANADA L7B 1A6
(905) 833-1244, FAX (05) 833-1255
wjr@lgl.com

Robilliard, Gordon
715 121st St., NW
Gig Harbor, WA 98332
(252) 858-2114
grobilliard@entrix.com

Rocque, Deborah
U.S. Fish and Wildlife Service
1011 E. Tudor Road, MS 331
Anchorage, AK 99503
(907) 786-3398, FAX (907) 786-3350
Deborah_rocque@fws.gov

Rockwell, Ted
U.S. EPA
222 W. 7th St.
Anchorage, AK 99513
(907) 271-3689, FAX (907) 271-3424
Rockwell.Theodore@epa.gov

Rodrigues, Bob
LGL Alaska Research Associates
1101 East 76th Ave.
Anchorage, AK 99518
(907) 562-3339

Rosen, Yereth
Reuters
3400 Purdue Street
Anchorage, AK 99508
(907) 349-4588, FAX (907) 349-4589
yjrosen@ak.net

Rothwell, Sally
ConocoPhillips Alaska, Inc.
700 G Street
Anchorage, AK 99501
(907) 265-6064, FAX (907) 265-1515
sally.a.rothwell@conocophillips.com

Rueffert, Celeste
Chief, Procurement Operations
Minerals Management Service
381 Elden Street, MS 2100
Herndon, VA 20170
(703)787-1324, FAX 787-1041
celeste.rueffert@mms.gov

Rotterman, Lisa
Alaska OCS Region
Minerals Management Service
3801 Centerpoint Drive, Suite 500
Anchorage, AK 99508
(907) 334-5245

Rugh, David*
National Marine Mammal Laboratory
Alaska Fisheries Science Center
7600 Sand Point Way, NE, F/AKC4
Seattle, WA 98115-6349
(206) 526-4018, FAX (206) 526-6615
david.rugh@noaa.gov

Saupe, Susan
Cook Inlet RCAC
910 Highland Ave.
Kenai, AK 99611
(907) 283-7222, FAX (907) 283-6102
saupe@circac.org

Savoie, Mark
Kinnetic Laboratories, Inc.
403 W. 8th Avenue
Anchorage, AK 99501
(907) 276-6178, FAX (907) 278-6881
msavoie@kinneticlabs.com

Schroeder, Willliam W.
MMS Scientific Advisory Committee University of
Alabama
101 Bienville Blvd.
Dauphin Island, AL 36528
(334) 861-7528, FAX (334) 861-7540
wschroeder@disl.org

Shea, Damian
NC State University
P.O. Box 7633, Toxicology
Raleigh, NC 27695
(919) 513-3899, FAX (919) 515-7169
d_shea@ncsu.edu

Sheehan-Dugan, Kathleen
State of Alaska
Natural Resources Dept.
550 W 7th Ave., Suite 1660
Anchorage, AK 99501
(907) 269-7474, FAX (907) 269-3981
kathy_dugan@dnr.state.ak.us

Smith, Caryn
Alaska OCS Region
Minerals Management Service
3801 Centerpoint Drive, Suite 500
Anchorage, AK 99508
(907) 334-5248, FAX (907) 334-5242
caryn.smith@mms.gov

Smith, Brad
National Marine Fisheries Service
222 W. 7th Street, Box 43
Anchorage, AK 99513
(907) 271-3023, FAX (907) 271-3030
brad.smith@noaa.gov

Snow, Norm
Inuvialuit Joint Secretariat
Box 2120
Inuvik, NT, X0E 0T0 CANADA
(867) 777-2828, FAX (867) 777-2610
execdir@jointsec.nt.ca

Somerville, Mark A.
ADNR-OHMP
HC60 Box 285B
Copper Center, AK 99573
(907) 269-6969
mark_somerville@dnr.state.ak.us

Sonsthagen, Sarah*
Institute of Arctic Biology
University of Alaska Fairbanks
227 Arctic Health
Fairbanks, AK 99775-7000
(907) 451-0247
ftsas@uaf.edu

Stapleton, Rob
ANI – Arctic Sounder
301 Calista Ct.
Anchorage, AK 99518
(907) 348-2463, FAX (907) 272-9512

Statscewich, Hank*
School of Fisheries and Ocean Sciences
University of Alaska Fairbanks
P.O. Box 757220
Fairbanks, AK 99775-7220

Stang, Paul*
Alaska OCS Region
Minerals Management Service
3801 Centerpoint Drive, Suite 500
Anchorage, AK 99508
(907) 334-5230

Streever, Bill
BP
4311 Edinburgh Drive
Anchorage, AK 99515
(907) 440-8324

Suydam, Robert*
Dept. of Wildlife Management
North Slope Borough
P.O. Box 69
Barrow, AK 99723
(907) 852-0350, FAX (907) 852-0351
Robert.Suydam@north-slope.org

Teller, Steve
P.O. Box 670454
Ohugiak, AK 99567
(907) 688-3916
teller@arctic.net

Thurston, Dennis
Alaska OCS Region
Minerals Management Service
3801 Centerpoint Drive, Suite 500
Anchorage, AK 99508
(907) 334-5338

Trefry, John*
Florida Institute of Technology
Division of Marine & Environmental Systems
150 W. University Blvd,
Melbourne, FL 32901
(321) 674-7305, FAX (321) 674-7212
jtrefry@fit.edu

Tremont, John
Alaska OCS Region
Minerals Management Service
3801 Centerpoint Drive, Suite 500
Anchorage, AK 99508
(907) 334-5261

Troy, Declan
Troy Ecological Research Assoc.
2322 E. 16th Ave.
Anchorage, AK 99508

Trudgen, Dave
Oasis Environmental
807 G Street
Anchorage, AK 99501
(907) 258-4880
dave@oasisenvir.com

Wang, Dong-Ping
Stony Brook University
Marine Sciences Center, Stony Brook University
Stony Brook, NY 11794
(631) 632-8691
dong-ping.wang@sunysb.edu

Wang, Jia*
IARC - University of Alaska
930 Koyukuk Dr., IARC Bldg., Rm 408F
Fairbanks, AK 99775-7335
(907) 474-2685, FAX (907) 474-2643
jwang@iarc.uaf.edu

Wedemeyer, Kate
Alaska OCS Region
Minerals Management Service
3801 Centerpoint Drive, Suite 500
Anchorage, AK 99508
(907) 334-5278

Williams, Dee
Alaska OCS Region
Minerals Management Service
3801 Centerpoint Drive, Suite 500
Anchorage, AK 99508
(907) 334-5283

Zhang, Sheng
IARC
2 Deadend Alley
Fairbanks, AK 99709
(907) 474-2684
szhang@irac.uaf.edu

* = Speaker

Bennett, James F.
Minerals Management Service
381 Elden Street
Herndon, VA 20170
(703) 787-1660, FAX (703) 787-1026
jfbennett@mms.gov

Braund, Stephen R.*
Stephen R. Braund and Associates
P.O. Box 1480
Anchorage, AK 99510
(907) 276-8222, FAX (907) 276-6117
srba@alaska.net

Brower, Jr., Arnold
North Slope Borough
P.O. Box 69
Barrow, AK 99723
(907) 852-0203

Cuyno, Leah *
Northern Economics, Inc.
880 H Street, Suite 210
Anchorage, AK 99501
(907) 274-5600, FAX (907) 274-5601
Leah.Cuyno@norecon.com

Downs, Mike*
EDAW, Inc.
1420 Kettner Blvd., Suite 620
San Diego, CA 92101
(619) 233-1454, FAX (619) 233-0952
downsm@edaw.com

Duguay, Claude*
Geophysical Institute
University of Alaska Fairbanks
Fairbanks, AK 99775
(907) 474-6832
claude.duguay@gi.alaska.edu

Duvall, Terra
IUM Assistant
MBC *Applied Environmental Sciences*
3000 Redhill Ave.
Costa Mesa, CA 92626
(714) 850-4830, FAX (714) 850-4840
tduvall@mbcnet.net

Elavqak, Michael
Allotment owner – Tashekpak area
P.O. Box 423
Barrow, AK 99723
(907) 852-5779

Galginaitis, Michael*
Applied Sociocultural Research
P.O. Box 101352
Anchorage, AK 99510-1352
(907) 272-6811, FAX (907) 222-6023
msgalginaitis@gci.net

George, J. Craig*
Department of Wildlife Management
North Slope Borough
P.O. Box 69
Barrow, AK 99723
(907) 852-0350

Hanns, Cyd
Department of Wildlife Management
North Slope Borough
P.O. Box 69
Barrow, AK 99723
(907) 852-0350, FAX (907) 852-0351
cyd.hanns@north-slope.org

Holder, Tim
ITM Coordinator
Alaska OCS Region
Minerals Management Service
3801 Centerpoint Drive, Suite 500
Anchorage, AK 99508
(907) 334-5279
Tim.Holder@mms.gov

Hopson, Charles
P.O. Box 172
Barrow, AK 99723
(907) 852-3212, FAX (907) 852-8213

Lampe, Doreen
North Slope Borough
Planning Department
P.O. Box 69
Barrow, AK 99723
(907) 852-0320, FAX (907) 852-0327
doreen.lampe@north-slope.org

McNeil, Paul
North Slope Borough
Planning Department/GIS
P.O. Box 69
Barrow, AK 99723
(907) 852-0333
paul.mcneil@north-slope.org

Mitchell, Chuck
President
MBC *Applied Environmental Sciences*
3000 Redhill Ave.
Costa Mesa, CA 92626
(714) 850-4830, FAX (714) 850-4840
cmitchell@mbcnet.net

Mitchell, Kathy
IUM Coordinator
MBC *Applied Environmental Sciences*
3000 Redhill Ave.
Costa Mesa, CA 92626
(714) 850-4830, FAX (714) 850-4840
kmitchell@mbcnet.net

Olemaun, George
North Slope Borough
P.O. Box 278
Barrow, AK 99723
golemaun@hotmail.com

Paquette, Carol
IUM Assistant
MBC *Applied Environmental Sciences*
3000 Redhill Ave.
Costa Mesa, CA 92626
(714) 850-4830, FAX (714) 850-4840
cpaquette@mbcnet.net

Patkotak, James
Inupiat Community of the Arctic Slope
P.O. Box 934
Barrow, AK 99723
(907) 852-4227, FAX (907) 852-4246
jcasnrd@starband.net

Prentki, Dick
Alaska OCS Region
Minerals Management Service
3801 Centerpoint Drive, Suite 500
Anchorage, AK 99508
(907) 334-5277

Rugh, David*
National Marine Mammal Laboratory
Alaska Fisheries Science Center
7600 Sand Point Way, NE, F/AKC4
Seattle, WA 98115-6349
(206) 526-4018, FAX (206) 526-6615
david.rugh@noaa.gov

Simmonds, Doreen
KBRW
P.O. Box 109
Barrow, AK 99723
(907) 852-6811

Suydam, Robert*
Dept. of Wildlife Management
North Slope Borough
P.O. Box 69
Barrow, AK 99723
(907) 852-0350, FAX (907) 852-0351
Robert.Suydam@north-slope.org

Williams, Waska Jr.
North Slope Borough
Planning Department
P.O. Box 69
Barrow, AK 99723
(907) 852-0440, FAX (907) 852-5991
waska.williams@north-slope.org